Contents

Introduction

Careers and Unemployment is Volume 263 in the **ISSUES** series. The aim of the series is to offer current, diverse information about important issues in our world, from a UK perspective.

ABOUT CAREERS AND UNEMPLOYMENT

Unemployment in Britain currently stands at 8.2% and many claim that there are simply no jobs available. But is this the case? Or are people simply unwilling to work? This book explores the debates surrounding benefits, financial security and 'worklessness'. It also looks at the crisis of youth unemployment, examining its causes and solutions. Finally, the third chapter of the book considers changing trends in the work-life balance of UK workers.

OUR SOURCES

Titles in the **ISSUES** series are designed to function as educational resource books, providing a balanced overview of a specific subject.

The information in our books is comprised of facts, articles and opinions from many different sources, including:

⇨ Newspaper reports and opinion pieces

⇨ Website factsheets

⇨ Magazine and journal articles

⇨ Statistics and surveys

⇨ Government reports

⇨ Literature from special interest groups

A NOTE ON CRITICAL EVALUATION

Because the information reprinted here is from a number of different sources, readers should bear in mind the origin of the text and whether the source is likely to have a particular bias when presenting information (or when conducting their research). It is hoped that, as you read about the many aspects of the issues explored in this book, you will critically evaluate the information presented.

It is important that you decide whether you are being presented with facts or opinions. Does the writer give a biased or unbiased report? If an opinion is being expressed, do you agree with the writer? Is there potential bias to the 'facts' or statistics behind an article?

ASSIGNMENTS

In the back of this book, you will find a selection of assignments designed to help you engage with the articles you have been reading and to explore your own opinions. Some tasks will take longer than others and there is a mixture of design, writing and research based activities that you can complete alone or in a group.

FURTHER RESEARCH

At the end of each article we have listed its source and a website that you can visit if you would like to conduct your own research. Please remember to critically evaluate any sources that you consult and consider whether the information you are viewing is accurate and unbiased.

Useful weblinks

www.adviceguide.org.uk

www.acevo.org.uk

www.cam.ac.uk

www.careerbuilder.co.uk

www.cass.city.ac.uk

www.cipd.co.uk

www.cps.org.uk

www.enterprisenation.com

www.esrc.ac.uk

www.flexibility.co.uk

www.headliners.org

www.highfliers.co.uk

www.ipsos.co.uk

www.jrf.org.uk

www.mckinsey.com

www.neweconomics.org

www.nhs.uk

Careers an

Series E

V

Independence Educational Publishers

First published by Independence Educational Publishers

The Studio, High Green

Great Shelford

Cambridge CB22 5EG

England

© Independence 2014

British Library Cataloguing in Publication Data

Careers and unemployment. -- (Issues ; 263)

1. Labor market--Great Britain. 2. Labor--Social

aspects--Great Britain.

I. Series II. Acred, Cara editor.

331.1'0941-dc23

ISBN-13: 9781861686787

Printed in Great Britain

MWL Print Group Ltd

Unemployment

What is unemployment?

Unemployment is an economic indicator that refers to the number or proportion of people in an economy who are willing and able to work, but are unable to get a job; a person in this situation is said to be unemployed. People who are not willing or able to work, for whatever reason, are 'economically inactive' and do not count towards unemployment figures.

High levels of unemployment are usually typical of a struggling economy, where labour supply is outstripping demand from employers. When an economy has high unemployment, it is not using its economic resources in the best possible way.

Unemployment also carries significant social costs. People who are unable to find work must frequently rely on benefits for income: if they have financial or family commitments, this can make life extremely difficult. Moreover, the sense of failure, boredom and rejection that being unemployed can generate has real social consequences. Studies have repeatedly linked unemployment to rising crime and suicide rates and the deterioration of health.

The causes of unemployment are manifold. Economists distinguish a number of types of unemployment, however: cyclical unemployment is brought about by the vagaries of the business cycle; structural unemployment is brought about by changes in the economy or the labour market, when the jobs available do not fit the workforce's skills; frictional unemployment is the phenomenon of people being 'between jobs'; and seasonal unemployment is linked to certain types of seasonal jobs, such as farm work and construction.

Background

The history of unemployment in the UK is central to both the economic and social history of the country.

The 1950s and 1960s saw a very low rate of unemployment (around three per cent on average) as a result of the 'postwar boom'. Servicemen during the Second World War had been promised full employment after victory, and no government of the period was prepared to break this pledge. Technological advance, a stable international trade environment, the success of Keynesian economics and the stability of the Phillips Curve (which postulated a relationship between high inflation and low unemployment) created a situation which did approach full employment – although of course, at that time the majority of women remained in the category of the 'economically inactive'.

The economic orthodoxies of the boom years collapsed in the 1970s. The energy crises of 1973 and 1979 generated 'stagflation', rising inflation and rising unemployment – something the Phillips Curve deemed impossible. In Europe, fixed exchange rates pegged to the German mark forced EU member states to deflate their economies to keep pace with low-inflation West Germany. The failure of Labour's 'In Place of Strife' labour market reform proposals in the late 1960s had led to a situation where union power was increasingly stifling markets by keeping wages high. Unemployment topped one million for the first time in January 1972. During the 1979 'Winter of Discontent', when even gravediggers went on strike to protest against pay freezes, unemployment stood at 1.1 million, and the Conservatives swept to power on the message that 'Labour isn't working'.

However, during the early 1980s, unemployment rose further still – it topped three million in 1982. The January 1982 figure of 3,070,621 represented 12.5 per cent of the working population, and in some parts of the country it was even higher: in Northern Ireland, unemployment

NO POSITIONS VACANT

NO JOB VACANCY

stood at 20 per cent, while in some areas dominated by declining industries such as coal mining, it was much higher still.

Unemployment began to fall again throughout the 1990s and by 1999 was below the two million mark at around 1.7 million. This trend continued until 2005 with official figures showing unemployment at 1.397 million. However, in the last two years of the Blair Government unemployment began to rise again and by 2008 Gordon Brown was coping with a global recession and unemployment figures back up to 1.79 million – the highest for a decade.

By the time the Coalition came to power in May 2010 unemployment had risen to over 2.5 million. The new Prime Minister, David Cameron, said unemployment was 'forecast to fall every year' under the Coalition's policies and he pledged: 'At the end of this Parliament unemployment will be falling.'

Unemployment continued to rise and official figures published in October 2011 showed that for the June to August quarter, 2.57 million people were unemployed – the highest since 1994.

This trend of rising unemployment continued through the last quarter of 2011 and the beginning of 2012, but there were increasing signs of stabilisation in the labour market and by March 2012, although unemployment showed a rise of 28,000 compared to the previous quarter, this was 5,000 below the headline figure of the previous month.

Then figures published in April 2012 showed the continuing rise in employment was coupled with a fall in unemployment of 35,000 on the quarter, to 2.65 million. This was despite the fact there were more people in the labour market, with a fall in inactivity of 25,000.

Figures for the March to May 2012 quarter also showed a continuing fall in unemployment. However, Employment Minister, Chris Grayling, said that whilst any fall in unemployment was very welcome, he remained 'cautious' about the next few months in light of the continuing economic challenges.

Controversies

Throughout history, policy-makers have from time to time taken the view that the macroeconomic benefits of high unemployment outweigh its economic and social costs. This was the case during the early 1980s. Most of the time, however, governments are unwilling to permit high unemployment, due to the demonstrated social effects, the economic underperformance it reflects and the public cost in terms of benefit payments it demands.

Nevertheless, as an aggregate figure the 'headline' unemployment figure and rate can only tell part of the story. Structural differences between the regions of the UK have often meant that a nationwide figure masks localised problems. For years, unemployment in the north of England, Scotland and Wales have been considerably higher

than in the prosperous South East and London. Even within regions, there are local pockets of high unemployment. Many towns remain dominated by a small number of large employers: when a locally-significant business closes, such as the mines during the 1980s or Rover's Longbridge plant in Birmingham more recently, the effect can be devastating.

Headline figures can also disguise other complexities, such as the prevalence of unemployment amongst ethnic minorities, women, disabled people, young people, and people who have been unemployed for long periods of time.

At present, there are two principal measures of unemployment used by the Government: the International Labour Organisation (ILO) measure (the UK's version being known as the Labour Force Survey or LFS unemployment); and the Claimant Count. The former is based on a survey of 57,000 households, and classifies participants as employed, unemployed or economically inactive on the basis of work done in the previous week. The latter is based on the numbers claiming unemployment-related benefits. On its election in 1997, the Labour Government proclaimed its preference for the ILO measure, because of its international recognition. However, it claimed that unemployment had fallen below one million in 2001 on the basis of the Claimant Count measure only: at that time, ILO unemployment stood at 1,535,000.

This is only the latest example of the problem of measuring unemployment. Most governments are keen to minimise the appearance of unemployment, not only for political reasons but also for the economic signals it sends out. Over the last 25 years, numerous revisions to the official definition of 'unemployment' have been made, which have almost universally revised it downwards. Labour frequently accused the Conservatives during the 1980s of moving unemployed people on to sickness benefits – classifying them as economically inactive rather than unemployed – as a strategy for cutting the unemployment figure.

In recent years, the problem of bringing more economically inactive people into the workforce has been rising on the political agenda across Europe. A 2000 study found that the economically active proportion of the population across the EU was just 69 per cent, around 77 million adults. The savings of the current workforce are increasingly believed to be insufficient to pay for the pensions of the soon-to-retire. Government has pursued this agenda by a combination of incentives, such as training and childcare, and sanctions, principally tightening eligibility for benefits such as Incapacity Benefit.

Following the publication of figures in October 2011 showing that unemployment had risen to 2.57 million, the leader of the Opposition, Ed Miliband, argued that as the Prime Minister had 'justified his economic policy' by saying unemployment would fall 'this year, next year and the year after', he must now 'change course so that he has a credible plan to get people back to work in this country'.

However, whilst acknowledging that the Government 'have to do more to get our economy moving and get jobs for our people', the Prime Minister remained adamant that 'we must not abandon the plan that has given us record low interest rates,' And he added: 'If we changed course on reducing our deficit, we would end up with interest rates like those in Portugal, Spain, Italy and Greece and we would send our economy into a tailspin.'

The Government's strategy appeared to be given credence by figures showing a continuing rise in employment from autumn 2011, accompanied by a fall in unemployment from early 2012, with reports of private sector job creation 'more than offsetting' the fall in public sector employment, as the Government had claimed.

Nevertheless, the TUC remained concerned that youth unemployment was not being addressed. General secretary Brendan Barber welcomed the unemployment figures published in July 2012, describing them as 'excellent news', but he pointed out that long-term youth joblessness was up by 18,000 on the quarter to 421,000, and urged the Government to prioritise tackling long-term youth unemployment. He also called for an increase in wage growth to help drive the economic recovery.

Statistics

Labour Force Survey – March to May 2012. The claimant count is for June 2012 and the vacancy count for April to June 2012.

The number of people in work rose this quarter:

⇨ 29.35 million people were in work in March to May 2012.

⇨ The employment level rose 181,000 on the previous quarter and 75,000 on the year.

⇨ The employment rate is 70.7%, up 0.3 points on the quarter but unchanged on the year.

ILO unemployment fell this quarter:

⇨ 2.58 million people were ILO unemployed in the March to May 2012 quarter, down by 65,000 on the December 2011 to February 2012 period but up 132,000 on the same quarter last year.

⇨ The ILO unemployment rate is 8.1%, down 0.2 percentage points on the quarter but up 0.4 percentage points on the year.

The level of economic inactivity is down on the quarter and on the year:

⇨ The economic inactivity level is 9.21 million, down 61,000 on the quarter and 121,000 on the year.

⇨ The economic inactivity rate is 22.9%, down 0.2 points on the quarter and 0.3 points on the year.

⇨ Excluding students, inactivity as a share of the 16–64 population is 17.4%, unchanged on the quarter but down 0.2 points on the year.

The number of people on JSA rose this month, but the number claiming one of the other main out-of-work benefits is improving:

⇨ Claimant unemployment was 1,604,000 in June 2012, up 6,100,000 thousand on the level in May 2012 and up 78,600,00 on the year.

⇨ The claimant unemployment rate, at 4.9%, is unchanged on the month but up 0.2 percentage points on the year.

⇨ The figures continue to be affected by welfare reform, including reforms to eligibility for lone parent benefits and re-assessment of existing claims for incapacity benefits. Both are likely to have added to the JSA caseload between May and June.

⇨ In the year to November 2011, the number claiming incapacity benefits fell 10,800 to 2.58 million. The most recent provisional figure for May 2012 suggests the caseload has since fallen further to 2.52 million.

⇨ In the year to November 2011, the number of lone parents on income support fell 66,700 to 581,600. The provisional figure for May 2012 is 575,000, suggesting the level is close to flat.

The number of redundancies fell and unfilled vacancies rose on the quarter:

⇨ There were 147,000 redundancies in March to May 2012, down 27,000 on the previous quarter but up 4,000 on the year.

⇨ ONS's vacancy survey estimates an average of 471,000 unfilled vacancies in the three months to June 2012, up 10,000 on the quarter and 12,000 on the year.

Total weekly pay in May 2012 was up by 1.5% over the year:

⇨ Growth in regular weekly pay, excluding bonuses, was up 1.8% on the year.

Source: Department for Work and Pensions – July 2012

⇨ The above information is reprinted with kind permission from Politics.co.uk. Please visit www.politics.co.uk for further information.

Rights at work

Your rights at work will depend on:

⇨ your statutory rights (see below), and

⇨ your contract of employment.

Your contract of employment cannot take away rights you have by law. So if, for example, you have a contract which states you are only entitled to two weeks' paid holiday per year when, by law, all full-time employees are entitled to 28 days' paid holiday per year, this part of your contract is void and does not apply. The right you have under law (to 28 days' holiday in this case) applies instead.

If your contract gives you greater rights than you have under law, for example, your contract gives you six weeks' paid holiday per year, then your contract applies.

There are special rules about the employment of children and young people.

Statutory rights

Statutory rights are legal rights based on laws passed by Parliament.

Nearly all workers, regardless of the number of hours per week they work, have certain legal rights. There are some workers who are not entitled to certain statutory rights.

Sometimes an employee only gains a right when they have been employed by their employer for a certain length of time. Unless you are in the group of workers who are excluded, you will have the following statutory rights:

⇨ the right to a written statement of terms of employment within two months of starting work.

⇨ the right to an itemised pay slip. This applies from the day the employee starts work.

⇨ the right to be paid at least the national minimum wage. This applies from the day the employee starts work.

⇨ the right not to have illegal deductions made from pay. This applies from the day the employee starts work.

⇨ the right to paid holiday. Full-time employees are entitled to at least 28 days a year. Part-time employees are entitled to a pro rata amount.

⇨ the right to time off for trade union duties and activities. This applies from the day the employee starts work. The time off does not necessarily have to be paid. Employees also have the right to be accompanied by a trade union representative to a disciplinary or grievance hearing. If an employee takes part in official industrial action and is dismissed as a result, this will be an automatic unfair dismissal.

⇨ the right to paid time off to look for work if being made redundant. This applies once the employee has worked for two years for that employer.

⇨ the right to time off for study or training for 16-17 year olds. This applies from the day the employee starts work .

⇨ the right to paid time off for ante natal care. This applies from the day the employee starts work.

⇨ the right to paid maternity leave. More on Maternity leave.

⇨ the right to paid paternity leave.

⇨ the right to ask for flexible working to care for children or adult dependents – see under heading The right to ask for flexible working.

⇨ the right to paid adoption leave.

⇨ the right to take unpaid parental leave for both men and women (if you have worked for the employer for one year) and the right to reasonable time off to look after dependants in an emergency (applies from the day the employee starts work) .

⇨ the right under Health and Safety law to work a maximum 48-hour working week. This applies from the day the employee starts work.

⇨ the right under Health and Safety law to weekly and daily rest breaks. This applies from the day the employee starts work. There are special rules for night workers.

⇨ the right not to be discriminated against. This applies from the day the employee starts work.

⇨ the right to carry on working until you are at least 65.

⇨ the right to notice of dismissal, provided you have worked for your employer for at least one calendar month.

⇨ the right to written reasons for dismissal from your employer, provided you have worked for your employer for one year if you started before 6 April 2012 or two years if you started on or after that date. Women who are pregnant or on maternity leave are entitled to written reasons without having to have worked for any particular length of time.

⇨ the right to claim compensation if unfairly dismissed. In most cases to be able to claim unfair dismissal you will have to have worked for your employer for one year if you started before 6 April 2012 or two years if you started on or after that date.

⇨ the right to claim redundancy pay if made redundant. In most cases you will have to have worked for two years to be able to claim redundancy pay.

⇨ the right not to suffer detriment or dismissal for 'blowing the whistle' on a matter of public concern (malpractice) at the workplace. This applies from the day the employee starts work.

⇨ the right of a part-time worker to the same contractual rights (pro-rata) as a comparable full-time worker.

⇨ the right of a fixed-term employee to the same contractual rights as a comparable permanent employee.

You may also have additional rights which may be set out in your contract of employment. In particular, a part-time worker's contract should be checked.

If in doubt about whether or not you have any statutory rights you should consult an experienced adviser, for example, at a Citizens Advice Bureau, To search for details of your nearest CAB, including those that can give advice by email, click on nearest CAB.

⇨ The above information is reprinted with kind permission from Citizens Advice. Please visit www.adviceguide.org.uk for further information.

© Citizens Advice 2014

The National Minimum Wage

What is the minimum wage?

The National Minimum Wage is the minimum pay per hour almost all workers are entitled to by law.

It doesn't matter how small an employer is, they still have to pay the minimum wage.

The minimum wage rate depends on a worker's age and if they're an apprentice.

Use the National Minimum Wage calculator to check if the minimum wage has been paid.

Workers can check if:

⇨ they're getting the minimum wage

⇨ an employer owes them payments from past jobs.

Employers can check if:

⇨ they're paying the minimum wage

⇨ they owe a worker payments from past jobs.

Who gets the minimum wage?

Entitled to the minimum wage

Workers must be school-leaving age (last Friday in June of the school year they turn 16) or over to get the minimum wage.

Contracts for payments below the minimum wage are not legally binding. The worker is still entitled to the minimum wage.

Workers are also entitled to the minimum wage if they are:

⇨ part-time

⇨ casual labourers, e.g. someone hired for one day

⇨ agency workers

⇨ workers and homeworkers paid by the number of items they make

⇨ apprentices

⇨ trainees, workers on probation

⇨ disabled workers

⇨ agricultural workers

⇨ foreign workers

⇨ seafarers

⇨ offshore workers.

Apprentices under 19 or in their first year get an apprentice rate.

Not entitled to the minimum wage

The following types of workers aren't entitled to the minimum wage:

⇨ self-employed people running their own business

⇨ company directors

⇨ volunteers or voluntary workers

⇨ workers on a government employment programme, e.g. the Work Programme

⇨ family members of the employer living in the employer's home

⇨ non-family members living in the employer's home who share in the work and leisure activities, are treated as one of the family

The National Minimum Wage rate per hour depends on your age and whether you're an apprentice – you must be at least school-leaving age to get it.				
Year	21 and over	18 to 20	Under 18	Apprentice*
2013 (current rate)	£6.31	£5.03	£3.72	£2.68
2012	£6.19	£4.98	£3.68	£2.65
2011	£6.08	£4.98	£3.68	£2.60
2010	£5.93	£4.92	£3.64	£2.50
*This rate is for apprentices under 19 or those in the first year of their apprenticeship.				

- t charged for meals or
  odation (e.g. au pairs)

- s younger than school-
  g age (usually 16)

⇨ higher and further education students on a work placement up to one year

⇨ workers on government pre-apprenticeship schemes

⇨ people on the following European Union programmes: Leonardo da Vinci, Youth in Action, Erasmus, Comenius

⇨ people working on a Jobcentre Plus Work trial for six weeks

⇨ members of the armed forces

⇨ share fishermen

⇨ prisoners

⇨ people living and working in a religious community.

Work experience and internships

You won't get the minimum wage if you're:

⇨ a student doing work experience as part of a higher or further education course

⇨ of compulsory school age

⇨ a volunteer or doing voluntary work

⇨ on a government or European programme

⇨ work shadowing

Voluntary work

You're classed as doing voluntary work if you can only get certain limited benefits (e.g. reasonable travel or lunch expenses) and you're working for a:

⇨ charity

⇨ voluntary organisation or associated fund-raising body

⇨ statutory body.

⇨ The above information is reprinted with kind permission from GOV.UK. Please visit www.gov.uk for further information.

© Crown copyright 2014

The age groups were different before 2010. There were no National Minimum Wage rates for apprentices.

Year	22 and over	18 to 21	Under 18
2009	£5.80	£4.83	£3.57
2008	£5.73	£4.77	£3.53
2007	£5.52	£4.60	£3.40
2006	£5.35	£4.45	£3.30
2005	£5.05	£4.25	£3.00

Benefits in Britain: separating the facts from the fiction

How many people are dependent on welfare – and do families where three generations have never worked really exist?

What percentage of the UK's adult population is dependent on the welfare state?

The welfare state is a big part of British family life, with 20.3 million families receiving some kind of benefit (64% of all families), about 8.7 million of them pensioners. For 9.6 million families, benefits make up more than half of their income (30% of all families), around 5.3 million of them pensioners. The number of families receiving benefits will be between one and two million fewer now because of changes to child tax credits that mean some working families who previously got a small amount now get nothing.

How big is the problem of families on benefits where generations have never worked?

The Joseph Rowntree Foundation published a study in December testing whether there were three generations of the same family that had never worked. Despite dogged searching, researchers were unable to find such families. If they exist, they account for a minuscule fraction of workless people. Under 1% of workless households might have two generations who have never worked – about 15,000 households in the UK. Families with three such generations will therefore be even fewer.

Importantly, families experiencing long-term worklessness remained

committed to the value of work and preferred to be in jobs rather than on benefits. There was no evidence of 'a culture of worklessness' – values, attitudes and behaviours discouraging employment and encouraging welfare dependence – in the families being passed down the generations. The long-term worklessness of parents in these families was a result of complex problems (particularly related to ill-health) associated with living in long-term and deep poverty. In an already tight labour market, multiple problems combined to place people at the back of a long queue for jobs.

For 2011–12 it is estimated that 0.8%, or £1.2 billion, of total benefit expenditure was overpaid as a result of fraud. This is far lower than the figures widely believed by the public, as revealed repeatedly in opinion polls. A TUC poll recently revealed that people believe 27% of the welfare budget is claimed fraudulently.

Hard to judge, and hard to generalise. There is a lot of movement in and out of work, so many Job Seekers Allowance claims are very short. More than 80% of claimants never go near the work programme because they aren't on the benefit for long enough. A lot are off it in under six months. For disability benefits, there are a lot more long-term claimants, of course. In 2012, 18% of working-age households were workless; in only 2% had no one ever worked. More than half of adults in households where no one has ever worked were under 25. So although the proportion of households where no one has ever worked has increased recently, it is likely to be a manifestation of high and rising young adult unemployment.

What proportion of the welfare bill goes on benefits to the unemployed? And how has this changed?

It's rising – but we've seen such movements before. At 13% between 2009–10 and 2011–12, the proportion of gross domestic product devoted to benefits is at an all-time high, but this is not the result of a long-term upward trend. Levels in the 1990s to 2008–09 fluctuated between 10% and 12%. The recession resulted in a substantial increase and the overall level has not fallen since. This mirrors the recession in the early 1990s, when the proportion of GDP spent on benefits increased by slightly more at around three percentage points.

Between 2001/02 and 2011/12, spending on 'social protection' benefits – help given to those in need or at risk of hardship – increased from £156 billion to £210 billion. This £54 billion growth was after inflation, a rate of 34%. At an increase of £24 billion, pensioner incomes made up the largest share of the change, around nine-tenths

of the growth, reflecting their size within the budget. Housing benefits spending grew at the fastest rate, 62%, because of increases in the number of claimants and the average cost of the benefit. Claimant numbers rose from 3.8 million in 2002 to five million in 2012, while average weekly benefit increased from £52 to £87.

If unemployment benefits are reduced, do more claimants find work?

They may stop claiming – but not necessarily go to work. The Joseph Rowntree Foundation has carried out a systematic review of international research on the impact of benefit sanctions. This finds, mainly from US research, that sanctions are successful in getting people off benefits, but this may be because they are dropping out of the system altogether, rather than going into decent work. European studies show that the use of sanctions is likely to lead to worse employment outcomes (lower pay and more likely to be back on benefits) than if sanctions are not used. This is because the threat or use of sanctions makes people take lower-quality jobs than if they had been allowed to wait for a better opportunity.

How many families last year received more in benefits than the proposed government cap of £26,000?

Around 58,000 households will have their benefits reduced by the policy in 2014–15. Greater numbers are affected by other welfare changes.

What proportion of people affected by the welfare reforms are in households where someone works?

It's not just the workless who will have to cut back. As the Institute for Fiscal Studies pointed out in January, because the proposed uprating changes apply to almost

all benefits and tax credits both work and out-of-work households are affected.

Out of 2.8 million workless households of working age, 2.5 million will see their entitlements reduced by an average of about £215 a year in 2015–16.

Of 14.1 million working-age households with someone in work, seven million will see their entitlements reduced, by an average of about £165 a year. Note that this figure includes three million families who lose only from the cuts to child benefit, at an average of about £75 a year. They also point out that other elements of the 'consolidation package' have different effects, particularly for those on higher incomes.

The impacts of other changes will also be very significant for working as well as out-of-work households. Joseph Rowntree Foundation research on the council tax benefit showed that 2.4 million low-income families will pay on average £138 more in council tax in 2013–14. About 78% of the 2.4 million affected live in non-working households and pay no council tax. The average additional payment will be £132 for in-work recipients and £140 for those not working.

What is the correlation between a country's economic performance and the size of its welfare bill?

Richer countries spend much more (as a proportion of income) on welfare than poor ones – compare Sweden and Somalia. But of course that doesn't mean spending more on welfare makes a country richer: it mostly reflects the natural tendency of societies, as they become more prosperous, to increase social spending. Some economists argue that large welfare states, which need to be financed by equally large tax revenues, over time inhibit private-sector growth. However, the experience of the Nordic countries does show clearly that there is no necessary inconsistency between economic dynamism and a large and relatively generous welfare state.

Perhaps a better way to think about it is this: it seems likely that having no welfare state would not only make a country a very unpleasant place to live in but would inhibit economic growth, as a consequence of the inevitable social breakdown; equally a country where the state taxed away everyone's income and redistributed it would have no incentives for economic activity. So there's unlikely to be one 'right answer'. In practice, what matters to growth is not so much the size of the welfare bill but how it is spent – what sort of incentives does it give to people to work, become trained or educated, and so on.

What does this tell us about the UK's welfare state and its impact on growth? In fact, the overall size of the welfare bill as a proportion of GDP has been fairly stable over the past quarter century.

To the extent there has been an upward trend, it's been driven by increasing numbers of pensioners, rather than more generous benefits. Meanwhile, spending on those below pension age – working age and children – has been flat overall, rising in recessions and falling outside them. And it's false to suggest that 'benefit dependency' has been steadily increasing; the number on out-of-work benefits (unemployment benefit, incapacity benefits and lone parents) peaked in the early 1990s and is now fully a million below that level.

This certainly doesn't tell us that spending is at the 'right' level. Indeed, most economists would agree that over time reforms – especially increasing state pension ages to reflect increasing life expectancy – are required to ensure long-term sustainability. But it does tell us that anyone who says that spending too much on welfare or benefits is the cause of the country's economic problems, or that spending less on them is the cure, is not paying much attention to the facts.

How many large families are heavily dependent on benefits?

To quote *The Economist*: 'Though most of them seem to end up in newspapers, in 2011 there were just 130 families in the country with ten children claiming at least one out-of-work benefit. Only 8% of benefit claimants have three or more children.

What evidence there is suggests that, on average, unemployed people have similar numbers of children to employed people ... it is not clear at all that benefits are a significant incentive to have children.'

How generous are our benefits in comparison to other EU countries?

Figures from Eurostat suggest the UK spends about the same as the EU average on unemployment and disability-related benefits, although it is behind the larger economies. The UK spends 12% less a head than France and 19% less than Germany, but almost twice as much as the Czech Republic.

How many have come off disability benefits since the reforms?

Since 2008, 878,000 new employment and support allowance claims have been closed before the claimant was able to be assessed and 729,000 have been found 'fit for work' by tests. Since May 2010, 527,000 employment and support allowance claims have been closed and 414,000 found 'fit for work'.

Do any families get more than £100,000 a year in benefits, as George Osborne has claimed?

A freedom of information request by Full Fact showed that in August 2010, there were fewer than five housing benefit claimants receiving the equivalent of £100,000 a year.

⇨ Compiled with help from the Joseph Rowntree Foundation; Full Fact; New Policy Institute; and Jonathan Portes, director, National Institute of Economic and Social Research.

6 April 2013

⇨ The above information is reprinted with kind permission from *The Guardian*. Please visit www.theguardian.com for further information.

...IT'S A JOB GETTING A JOB...

VACA

Simplifying the welfare system and making sure work pays

Issue

Many people on benefits believe that the financial risks of moving into work are too great. For some, the gains from work, particularly if they work part-time, are small, and any gain can easily be cancelled out by costs such as transport.

The Government believes that the current system is too complex and there are insufficient incentives to encourage people on benefits to start paid work or increase their hours.

We are aiming to make the benefit system fairer and more affordable to help reduce poverty, worklessness and welfare dependency and to reduce levels of fraud and error.

Actions

We are reforming the welfare system to help more people to move into and progress in work, while supporting the most vulnerable.

Introducing Universal Credit

We are introducing Universal Credit in 2013 for people who are looking for work or on a low income. Universal Credit brings together a range of working-age benefits into a single payment. It will:

⇨ encourage people on benefits to start paid work or increase their hours by making sure work pays

⇨ smooth the transitions into and out of work

⇨ simplify the system, making it easier for people to understand, and easier and cheaper to administer

⇨ reduce the number of people who are in work but still living in poverty

⇨ reduce fraud and error.

Introducing Personal Independence Payment

Disability Living Allowance (DLA) is a tax-free benefit for children and adults who need help with personal care or their mobility needs. It was introduced in 1992 and had not been fundamentally reviewed or reformed since. There is confusion about the purpose of the benefit, it is complex to claim and there is no systematic way of checking that awards remain correct.

We have introduced a new benefit called Personal Independence Payment (PIP) from 8 April 2013 that will eventually replace DLA for people aged 16 to 64. PIP helps towards some of the extra costs because of a long-term ill-health condition or disability. It's based on how a person's condition affects them, not the condition they have. It's designed to be a more sustainable benefit and make sure support continues to reach those who face the greatest challenges to taking part in everyday life.

Introducing the Jobseeker's Allowance Claimant Commitment

From 14 October 2013 we are introducing a new Claimant Commitment that outlines what jobseeking actions a claimant must carry out while receiving Jobseeker's Allowance. The Claimant Commitment is due to be in place across the country by spring 2014 and brings Jobseeker's Allowance into line with claimants' responsibilities under Universal Credit.

Introducing a cap on the amount of benefits working-age people can receive

From 2013 we will introduce a cap on the total amount of benefits that working-age people can receive so that households on working-age benefits can no longer receive more in benefits than the average wage for working families.

Reassessing incapacity benefits recipients for Employment and Support Allowance

Employment and Support Allowance (ESA) replaced a range of incapacity benefits in 2008 for customers making a new claim because of illness or incapacity.

From October 2010, those people who are still receiving the older style incapacity benefits are being reassessed and moved to ESA or other benefits more appropriate to their circumstances. This exercise will continue until 2014.

Improving the Work Capability Assessment

Anyone claiming ESA will have a Work Capability Assessment to assess their capability for work. To ensure that the Work Capability Assessment is as fair and accurate as possible, we are continuing to review and improve it.

Making sure housing support is fair and affordable

We are creating a fairer approach to the way we pay housing costs to help bring stability to the housing market and improve incentives for people to find work or increase their hours.

From April 2013 we have introduced new rules for the size of accommodation that Housing Benefit, and then Universal Credit, will cover for working-age tenants renting in the social sector. This makes the rules consistent with those that apply to tenants renting in the private rented sector.

Increasing penalties for benefit fraud

We introduced tougher penalties for people who commit benefit fraud in the Welfare Reform Act 2012. From April 2013, the changes affect when benefit can be reduced or stopped as a penalty and how penalties increase for persistent offenders.

January 2014

⇨ The above information is reprinted with kind permission from the Department for Work & Pensions. Please visit www.gov.uk for further information.

No jobs? Or are British workers unwilling to take some of them?

By Ryan Bourne

'There are no jobs'. How many times have you heard it? It's a phrase repeated on practically every discussion programme on the economy, on every channel, every day.

Yet I've spent the past two days talking to UK fruit farmers, and many of them tell me they constantly advertise for seasonal UK labour. The response? Pitiful.

Take S&A Produce. In 2009 they advertised 2,000 seasonal jobs for their strawberry picking season in Herefordshire, but got just 12 applications from British nationals. At the time, 8% of the county's 16–24 year olds were claiming Jobseekers' Allowance. Three farmers from Kent regularly advertise early each year, but barely get any responses. 'And even if we did,' one told me, 'many British people who come down don't last more than a couple of days.'

Recently the MP for Sheppey and Sittingbourne, Gordon Henderson, ran a Westminster Hall Debate to discuss this. Numerous members, from those in constituencies in the West Midlands, to Scotland and Northern Ireland, all lined up in broad consensus that the fruit farming industry was now ultra-dependent on immigrant labour.

With unemployment at 8.2% across the country, and youth unemployment at 21.9%, this should both surprise and worry us. Why is it that British people are unwilling or unable to take this work?

This was the context for a debate which I participated in this morning on BBC Radio Kent. At the Kent County Show today, the Secretary of State for the Environment, Caroline Spelman, will be lobbied by the National Farmers Union to develop a new initiative to replace the Seasonal Agricultural Workers Scheme (SAWS). With plummeting interest in seasonal horticultural work in the UK, the UK Border Force have for years run the scheme, which has allowed farmers and growers in the UK to recruit low-skilled overseas workers to do short-term agricultural work on a quota basis. Farmers and growers can employ a fixed number of overseas workers through the scheme every year. The workers are given short-term work cards, with a maximum stay of six months.

Initially the scheme applied to students from outside of the European Union. But with the accession of Romania and Bulgaria to the EU, and the desire to impose transitional controls on these countries, the scheme has been opened exclusively to nationals of these countries since 2008. In 2012 and 2013, as many as 21,250 migrants from these countries will come across to pick our fruit each year. But from 2014, when the people of the two countries will be granted completely free movement within the single market, the farmers are worried that the appeal of picking fruit will be diminished, and the migrants will seek other better-paid jobs. They therefore want a new scheme which brings in workers from even further afield to guarantee their supply of labour.

The Government, for its part, is obviously not keen on this. It has huge political capital invested in bringing down immigration numbers, and has made great play on eliminating 'unskilled immigration' from outside of the EU, and so will be unwilling to make an exception for one industry. It's difficult not to think the farmers are overstating their case. The wage the Romanian/Bulgarian workers could receive here for fruit-picking – a minimum wage set by the Agricultural Wage board – will still be three or four times higher than wages available back home, making it difficult to see why supply of labour should be a problem (particularly with Europe-wide unemployment so high). One suspects this is more about the convenience for the farmers.

Nevertheless, this mustn't allow us to ignore the basic fact: these are at least 20,000 jobs (far more when you consider other migrants from within the EU) which British workers seem unwilling to undertake, despite the fact they offer minimum wages and accommodation – so aren't undercutting potential low-skilled employees.

Welfare is undoubtedly an important factor here. The withdrawal of benefits leaves individuals facing significant marginal effective tax rates, reducing the incentive to take the work. This becomes even more of a problem when the system is geared towards people finding full-time work, making coming on and off of benefits more difficult, and a problem that the Universal Credit will hopefully nullify by increasing disregarded income from 2013.

Several Conservative MPs have therefore suggested welfare reform alone will encourage more Brits to take up work on our farms. But the tax and benefit system can't be the only explanation. Most of the farmers claim that the Romanian and Bulgarian workers are more flexible, more hard-working and more productive. This is partly a consequence of the wage differential between the two countries, which is so large that economics graduates such as Ababi Mircea from Romania feel that they are better off

utilising their talents productively in this line of work. 'The money I make here in one week I make in Romania in one month,' he recently told the BBC. Is it therefore any surprise that farmers would rather take on enthused high-skilled workers?

That we don't seem to see the same drive and enthusiasm from indigenous people in fruit picking is evidence of a broader issue as countries get richer. Increasing wealth changes people's aspirations, and there now appears to be a snobbishness against taking work as a fruit-picker, even from those with low skills and little in the way of employment prospects. This is not unique to the UK. On a recent trip to Malaysia, I was struck by the number of Bangladeshis working on palm oil plantations in jobs which even the middle-income Malaysians were seemingly unwilling to do. But for countries as rich as us, this seems even more acute. Whereas many relatively wealthy young people may previously have picked fruit in the summer, they now aspire to go trekking in Borneo or to, dare I say it, pick fruit in Australia.

It's important to bear this in mind next time you see a debate in which someone claims there are no jobs. There are, but often we appear unwilling to take them. Welfare reform

will help at the margins, but the eagerness and vigour with which the Romanian and Bulgarian migrants take to their task shows the hunger for betterment that perhaps we have lost (and used to have when hundreds of families spent their summer holidays doing it).

Two other key lessons seem apt here: the divide between low-skilled and high-skilled immigration is simplistic and misleading – in this instance, the arrival of pickers has aided the UK economy and in the future a cap on skilled migrants will be a crude way of maintaining support for control of the borders. Second, for the unemployed, fruit picking might seem a menial task, but it could be an important rung on the job ladder. The fact that graduates travel hundreds of miles to do it shows there's nothing to be ashamed of.

13 July 2013

⇨ The above information is reprinted with kind permission from the Centre for Policy Studies. Please visit www.cps.org.uk for further information.

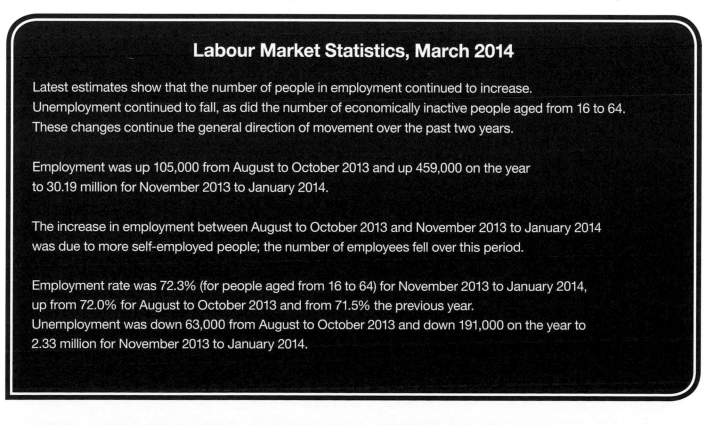

Labour Market Statistics, March 2014

Latest estimates show that the number of people in employment continued to increase.
Unemployment continued to fall, as did the number of economically inactive people aged from 16 to 64.
These changes continue the general direction of movement over the past two years.

Employment was up 105,000 from August to October 2013 and up 459,000 on the year
to 30.19 million for November 2013 to January 2014.

The increase in employment between August to October 2013 and November 2013 to January 2014
was due to more self-employed people; the number of employees fell over this period.

Employment rate was 72.3% (for people aged from 16 to 64) for November 2013 to January 2014,
up from 72.0% for August to October 2013 and from 71.5% the previous year.
Unemployment was down 63,000 from August to October 2013 and down 191,000 on the year to
2.33 million for November 2013 to January 2014.

We need full employment to curb *Benefits Street* wealth gap

An article from The Conversation.

By Clare Bambra, Professor of Public Health Policy in the Department of Geography at Durham University and Kayleigh Garthwaite, Postdoctoral Research Associate in the Department of Geography at Durham University

In a new report, *Working For The Few*, Oxfam warns that the fight against poverty cannot be won until wealth inequality has been tackled. The wealth of the richest 1% in the world amounts to $110 trillion – or 65 times as much as the poorest half of the world, says Oxfam, which fears this concentration of economic resources is threatening political stability and driving up social tensions.

The world's richest 85 people, who could all fit on a double decker bus, own as much as the world's poorest 3.5 billion. You couldn't get a clearer picture of wealth inequality – except, perhaps, if that bus were to draw up outside James Turner Street, the deprived subject of Channel 4's fly-on-the-wall documentary *Benefits Street* which is attracting huge attention, prompting protests and eliciting outrage from members of the public, MPs and charities.

The really divisive thing about the levels of wealth inequality portrayed by *Benefits Street* and our double-decker of plutocrats and oligarchs is that the bleak poverty tends to pit the very poorest people against each other, instead of the system that keeps them poor – or the people who live in almost unbelievable luxury while others struggle to make ends meet.

As *Benefits Street* so clearly illustrates, William Beveridge's five giant evils – squalor, ignorance, want, idleness, and disease – are alive and well in England today. Overcrowded, poor-quality housing is occupied by human beings battling malnutrition as they try to live on incomes of £30–60 per week (or in some cases no income at all), while facing regular eviction threats. And those who find work more often than not have to endure long hours and exploitation by gang masters.

There is also resilience and hope in the form of a strong community spirit, mutual help and support, the involvement of the local church, and the desire expressed by participants for a better future and for work. Yet *Benefits Street* downplayed these positives so as to add to the growing number of media representations of 'poverty porn', which portrays benefits recipients as 'shirkers and scroungers', wilfully languishing on benefits at the taxpayers' expense.

Research regularly shows the difficulties faced by people on benefits, their fear of sanctions, the difficulties they face in getting work in an economy that does not provide enough jobs, and the health consequences of worklessness (in terms of diet, alcohol, tobacco and substance abuse but also mental health and, eventually, mortality).

Lack of work in our society underpins the problems demonstrated in *Benefits Street*, and research shows it is also the root cause of long-term issues such as health inequalities. Areas with higher employment rates have better health and longer life expectancy, better housing and schools, and more besides. The social determinants of health were demonstrated very clearly in *Benefits Street*: now it is time to do something about them.

We need to tackle the societal barriers first and then the individual ones, since policy has focused too much on the latter and too little on the former. We need a benefits system that does not penalise work, and which does not penalise those without work by sanctioning them: we cannot starve people into jobs that don't exist. There are two-sides to 'making work pay' – it cannot simply be about cutting benefits – we also need an economy that actually provides work with living wages, and proper regulation of employers and landlords. We need a system that works for people, not just profit.

We used to have this in Britain. Full employment was one of the central principles of the post-war consensus and the basis of Beveridge's welfare state. Rents and landlords were properly regulated and there was a large, high-quality social housing stock. But the political elite has abandoned this since the 1980s, when unemployment was considered to be 'a price worth paying' for lower inflation, council housing stock was sold off, the regulation of landlords was 'relaxed' and employment rights were curtailed.

We need to remake this social commitment as responsibilities for work cut both ways. There has been too much focus on the responsibilities of individuals and too little on those of society. As a society we have the responsibility to provide work by creating and sustaining good-quality jobs and providing the training and support necessary to obtain them. We also have the responsibility to look after those who cannot work (for example, because of poor health). Only then will we make poverty history in the UK.

23 January 2014

⇨ The above information is reprinted with kind permission from The Conversation Trust (UK). Please visit www.theconversation.com for further information.

Are 'cultures of worklessness' passed down the generations?

This report critically investigates the idea of 'intergenerational cultures of worklessness' and that there may be families where 'three generations have never worked'.

By Tracy Shildrick, Robert MacDonald, Andy Furlong, Johann Roden and Robert Crow

This research was undertaken with families in neighbourhoods of Glasgow and Middlesbrough who had experienced extensive worklessness. Qualitative life-history interviews with different generations of the same family allowed us to investigate the extent to which long-term detachment from the labour market might be accounted for by a 'culture of worklessness'.

The aims and background of the research

The idea that worklessness can be explained, at least in part, by the familial inheritance of values and practices that discourage employment and encourage welfare dependency, is a powerful one. Indeed, much UK policy thinking continues to be based on the premise that workless people can become dependent on welfare and that this dependence is passed on between different generations within families, particularly in neighbourhoods where high rates of worklessness prevail. Through a critical case study approach, using methods and research sites most likely to reveal 'intergenerational cultures of worklessness', the project put these ideas to the test.

'Three generations who have never worked'

Social statistics suggest that the proportion of workless households with two generations who have never worked is very small – approximately half of one per cent of workless households. Despite dogged searching in localities with high rates of worklessness across decades we were unable to locate any families in which there were three generations in which no-one had ever worked. Although we know of no other studies that have explicitly sought to measure or research families where 'three generations have never worked', if such families do exist, logically they will be even fewer in number than those estimated to have two-generational worklessness (i.e. an even more minuscule fraction of workless families). Eventually, we recruited 20 families where there was:

⇨ a parent in the middle generation (aged between late 30s and mid-50s) who had experienced very long-term worklessness (defined as currently being out of work and having been so for at least the last five years – although many had been out of work for longer than this)

⇨ at least one child of working age (typically aged 16 to mid-20s) who was unemployed (most of whom had never had a job).

The difficulties in recruiting this sample, and the need to relax our initial recruitment criteria to do so, corroborates available statistical evidence showing long-term, cross-generational worklessness in households to be a rare phenomenon.

The typical story for the majority in this middle generation was of leaving school and entering employment relatively easily. Despite this early engagement with the labour market, when interviewed, these mid-aged interviewees all had long histories of worklessness. We met two people in the middle generation who had never had a job (recent research tells us that there are no more than 20,230 families in the UK where two generations have never worked).

Rarely were there simple explanations for why individuals in the middle generation had such extensive records of worklessness. Typically, a range of problems associated with social exclusion and poverty combined to distance people from the labour market. These problems included, but were not limited to:

⇨ poor schooling and educational underachievement

⇨ problematic drug and alcohol use

⇨ the attraction of opportunities in illicit economies (such as drug dealing) when legitimate opportunities were scarce

⇨ criminal victimisation

⇨ offending and imprisonment

⇨ domestic violence, and family and housing instability

⇨ physical and mental ill health.

Children of those with extensive worklessness in this middle generation comprised the younger generation of the sample (and were typically aged 16 to their mid-20s). Most of the younger generation had never been employed. Whilst emphatically not occupying 'a culture of worklessness', they carried the disadvantages of being brought up in largely workless households with multiple problems (such as having spent time in local authority care, having faced housing moves that disrupted their education, and lacking the family social and cultural capital that can help people into jobs). Nevertheless, they clung to conventional values and aspirations about jobs. Members of their wider family and social networks who were in employment acted as role models and sources of inspiration to these young people. The main explanation for their worklessness was that they were attempting to make their transitions into the labour market in a period of national economic downturn, and of high national and very high rates of local unemployment.

'Cultures of worklessness'

Theories about cultures of worklessness suggest that people are unemployed because of their values, attitudes and behaviours rather than because of a shortage of jobs. In simple terms, they imply people prefer a life on welfare benefits to working for a living. A theory of 'intergenerational cultures of worklessness' adds to this by arguing that such values, behaviours and attitudes are transmitted in families, from unemployed parents to their children who, in turn, pass on anti-employment and pro-welfare dependency attitudes to their own children. Over time, these cultures of worklessness become entrenched and are said to explain the persistent, concentrated worklessness that can be found in some British towns and cities.

We found no evidence to support the idea that participants were part of a culture of worklessness, and none for the idea of intergenerational cultures of worklessness. Despite their long-term worklessness, parents actively strove for better for their children and often assisted them in searching for jobs. Young people in these families described wanting to avoid the poverty, worklessness and other problems that had affected their parents. Running directly counter to theories of intergenerational cultures of worklessness, the research found that conventional, mainstream attitudes to and values about work were widespread in both the middle and younger generations. Employment was understood to offer social, psychological and financial advantages (compared with worklessness and a reliance on benefits). Interviewees knew it was better to be in work than to be out of work, partly because of the deep and long-term poverty that extensive worklessness had brought to these families.

The interviewees did not occupy social or family networks that were isolated from employment or from working cultures. Inevitably, given the localities we studied, unemployment was common in their family and social networks – but, so was employment. Even in the very deprived neighbourhoods we studied, most working-age residents were in jobs. A telling finding (against the cultures of worklessness thesis) was the variability of work histories in the families we studied. Employed family members (e.g. other siblings or members of the extended family) sometimes served as role models or provided inspiration, especially to younger interviewees. We found very little evidence of people working fraudulently, 'on the side' whilst in receipt of benefits, which is claimed to be another facet of cultures of worklessness. Many in the sample did 'work', however, if we use the term to mean something more than paid employment. The work of looking after children in very difficult circumstances and caring for other relatives, meant that some women (and it was women rather than men in the main) were limited in their opportunities to engage with employment. Volunteering was not uncommon in the sample; for people with limited labour market opportunities, voluntary work has been found to provide some of the positive social and psychological benefits of employment. Finally, some individuals became involved with criminal work, particularly shoplifting and drug dealing, usually to fund their own dependent drug use.

Conclusions

The study concludes that the notion of three or even two generations of families where no-one has ever worked is ill-founded as an explanation for contemporary worklessness in the UK. Such families account for a vanishingly small fraction of the workless. Our research shows that the more general idea of 'intergenerational cultures of worklessness' is also an unhelpful concept in trying to understand patterns of extensive worklessness in families.

We would stress that the sample of families in our study is extremely unusual. Their histories of very lengthy worklessness are typical neither of working-class people in Glasgow and Teesside, nor of other people living in poverty and experiencing worklessness. Other research has shown that a pattern of churning between low-paid jobs and unemployment is likely to be a more common experience. What makes them unusual and explains their distance from the labour market is the sheer preponderance of hardships and problems in their lives. The report concludes that politicians and policy-makers should abandon the idea of intergenerational cultures of worklessness – and, indeed, of cultures of worklessness. These ideas failed to explain even the extreme cases of prolonged worklessness we uncovered so they are unlikely to capture more common and widespread experiences of worklessness.

December 2012

⇨ The above information is reprinted with kind permission from the Joseph Rowntree Foundation. Please visit www.jrf.org.uk for further information.

A woman's work is never done?

One of the greatest social changes across Europe in recent decades has been the increase of women in the labour market. However, changes in women's work patterns have not always been matched by changes in the division of household tasks between the sexes, reveals a study from the European Social Survey (ESS).

So, perhaps not unfairly, women often feel their work is never done, with those working full-time still responsible, on average, for around two-thirds of the total time heterosexual couples spend on housework. However, with women doing most of the housework this can lead to feelings of work–life conflict – for men!

The 'double-burden' of paid and domestic work on women's experiences of work–family conflict was also explored, which found that despite the added burden of being responsible for most of the housework, women in these countries working full-time did not experience greater feelings of work–life conflict than men working similar hours. In fact, these findings from a large study by the ESS suggest that it may be men rather than women who have the most to gain from a more equal distribution of housework between the sexes.

Northern European men whose female partners did most of the housework were more likely to experience work–family conflict, compared with men who took on a larger share of the housework. Perhaps men in this situation feel guilty for not doing their fair share or perhaps the unequal division of household tasks creates tension between them and their partner?

⇨ It is still common for women to do the majority of housework, even when they hold down a full-time job.

⇨ The distribution of household labour is most equal in Nordic countries and least equal in southern Europe.

⇨ In the UK, 70 per cent of all housework is done by women and still nearly two-thirds of all housework is done by women even if they work over 30 hours per week.

⇨ In Greece, over 80 per cent of all housework is done by women and for those women working 30 hours or more per week, more than three-quarters of them still have responsibility for household chores.

⇨ Swedish women seem to have the most helpful partners with only two-thirds of all housework done by women, and this figure improves again if they are working more than 30 hours per week.

These are some insights into attitudes on moral and social issues that have been revealed in newly published findings from the ESS and shows that significant differences between countries still remain despite closer European integration.

ESS, whose fieldwork in the UK has been funded by the Economic and Social Research Council (ESRC), has collected data from more than 250,000 interviews in 30 countries over the last decade on a wide range of topics that tap into key issues facing contemporary Europe. These include people's experience of working in a recession, welfare state, political participation, immigrants' civic participation, fear of crime, well-being, ageism and homosexuality.

Paul Boyle, Chief Executive of ESRC, commented: 'This latest selection of findings from the European Social Survey (ESS) provides a valuable insight into attitudinal and behavioural trends across Europe. Despite the closer integration of these countries through the European Community, it highlights that significant differences remain. Only through the production of such rigorous, cross-national data will key stakeholders and policy makers be able to interpret how the social, political and moral fabric is not only changing within individual countries but also throughout Europe as a whole.'

> **'One of the greatest social changes across Europe in recent decades has been the increase of women in the labour market'**

Director of the ESS, Rory Fitzgerald, said: 'The European Social Survey has been measuring social attitudes and behaviour across Europe for just over a decade. The data paints a fascinating picture of the differences and similarities across Europe and highlights important regional variation. For instance the Great Recession has led to a growing economic and political gap between North and South, whilst attitudes towards homosexuality have become more polarised between East and West. The ESS Findings Booklet reminds us that there are many social, economic and moral differences between the countries and regions of Europe.'

Six ESS surveys have now been conducted, carried out every two years and covering more than 30 countries throughout Europe. Further rounds are planned to paint an accurate picture of European attitudes.

The UK has led the ESS's application for ERIC status, on behalf of 15 countries. The European Commission's decision setting up the ESS ERIC is anticipated shortly.

23 July 2013

⇨ The above information is reprinted with kind permission from ESRC. Please visit www.esrc.ac.uk for further information.

UK workers less financially secure today than in Thatcher's Britain

Today's employees are more likely to fall into financial difficulty than they were 30 years ago, according to a new report from Cass Business School, part of City University London. The UK workforce has changed dramatically, becoming older, more feminised and including more disabled workers. But, employee benefits – designed to provide financial protection – have failed to adapt, leaving workers financially exposed.

In 1979, we elected our first female Prime Minister, but by 2012 women represented more than half the UK workforce. According to *Keeping Pace? Financial Insecurity in the Modern Workforce*, commissioned by Income Protection provider Unum, there are 46% more older workers and 11% more workers who are ill or disabled, when compared to Thatcher's Britain.

The same period saw the introduction of the first mobile phone – practically a stone age device compared with today's smartphones – and both the birth and death of the CD. However, employee benefits provision, including pensions and Income Protection, haven't kept pace with change, resulting in a workforce that is less financially secure now than 30 years ago.

The report shows that workers in financial difficulty are less productive, and says it's in an employer's best interests to better protect their staff.

The report identifies three groups that are most 'at risk' due to the likelihood of periods of unemployment: people with disabilities or long-term illnesses, older workers and employees with caring responsibilities. It finds that women are more likely to fall into one of the 'at risk' categories, meaning that they are disproportionately impacted by the employee benefits gap.

People with disabilities or long-term illnesses

This group is more likely to fall into unemployment, and to struggle to re-enter the workplace. And, the number of people with disabilities or long-term illnesses has increased by 11%.

The report recommends that employers:

⇨ Provide specialist vocational support to help employees return to work

⇨ Offer Income Protection to increase financial security when long-term sick, and allow employees to maintain their standard of living while unable to work

⇨ Make workplace adaptations to both help people remain in employment, and to help people back to work.

Older workers

By 2020, a third of the UK's workforce will be over 50. Yet the report finds that workers are increasingly under-prepared for old age and ill-prepared to support themselves in retirement.

The report recommends that employers:

⇨ Partner with insurers to develop and offer group social care protection to help employees meet the first £75,000 of care costs

⇨ Contribute a higher proportion of salaries to workplace pension schemes

⇨ Provide higher contributions to women, to address gender inequalities caused by career breaks to have children and the increased likelihood of flexible working.

Employees with caring responsibilities

There are a greater number of employees who have caring responsibilities for both children and older relatives – usually women. Past research shows that 15% of people leave work within a year of their spouse becoming unemployed for health reasons.

The report recommends that employers:

⇨ Extend flexible working rights to older people and those with

caring responsibilities, to allow them to remain in work

⇨ Provide elective medical insurance, to speed up recovery for this group, as illness can prevent people from carrying out caring responsibilities – impacting on dependents.

Keeping Pace? Financial Insecurity in the Modern Workforce states that by better supporting these groups, employers can improve employee well-being and productivity.

Peter O'Donnell, CEO of Unum UK, said: 'More than ever, people are looking to their employers to provide the financial protection they need. A better protected workforce is good for the employer, as well as the employee.

'From our experience, we know that employees with the rehabilitation support that comes with Income Protection find it easier to transition back to work, should they leave the workforce.'

Cass Professor Nick Bacon commented: 'Financial insecurity has been compounded by an increased cost of living and higher levels of unemployment, meaning that employees are more likely to fall into financial difficulty than they were 30 years ago. During the same period, employee benefits have declined, leaving a gaping hole in the financial protection of today's employees.

'Financial insecurity has a negative impact on employee health and well-being, and also productivity. Employers that provide benefits designed to support the financial security of their staff, such as access to vocational rehabilitation, typically see a more productive workforce.'

7 June 2013

⇨ The above information is reprinted with kind permission from the Cass Business School. Please visit www.cass.city. ac.uk for further information.

What's in a name?

Flexible, Smart, Agile ... what should we call the new ways of working transforming the workplace?

Foreword from the book Smart Flexibility, *by Andy Lake*

That the world of work is changing is undeniable. But how should we refer to the new and flexible working practices that are evolving?

There are many words and phrases used to describe the changes: Flexible Working, New Ways of Working, Agile Working and Smart Working are the most commonly used phrases. For aspects of the new ways that use technology to work beyond the workplace there are words and phrases like Telework, Telecommuting, eWork, Location Independent Working, Workshifting and several others besides.

And sometimes flexible working is presented as being synonymous with 'Family Friendly Working' to emphasise the role of these new ways in assisting work–life balance. Often these are linked with options like maternity and paternity leave. This is quite a dominant mode of thought in some of the HR literature, academic research and some government policy areas, but it is really too narrow and lacks sufficient business focus to be widely accepted.

So at the outset, I think I should begin by outlining what it is I mean by the term 'Smart Flexibility'.

Flexible Working and Smart Working

'Flexible Working' in an organisation encompasses:

⇨ a range of flexible working practices

⇨ changes to the way work is carried out and services are delivered

⇨ changes to the environments in which work is carried out.

Flexible working practices typically fall into three areas:

⇨ Flexible time options – such as flexitime or variable hours, compressed working week (doing five days work in four, or ten days in nine, etc.), annualised hours, part-time working, job share, term-time working

⇨ Flexible location options – such as mobile working, home-based working, working seamlessly from other company sites or from client sites, working from local 'work hubs'

upon which young people are particularly dependent for work, and then with the 2008 recession across the economy as a whole. The immediate crisis will therefore only be resolved through stronger labour market demand. We do not enter the macroeconomic debate about the speed and scale of the Government's deficit and debt reduction programme. But for any given level of overall demand in the economy, we need to shift the odds for young people. The Government have recognised the principle with a proposal to subsidise employers who take on young people. To make a real dent in unemployment, we need bigger and more incentives sooner. The 'bazooka' needs to be big enough for the task. We call for the Youth Contract to be front-loaded, thereby doubling the number of job subsidies available in 2012, and for young people on the Work Programme for a year to be guaranteed a part-time 'First Step' job as a stepping stone to unsupported employment.

Young people need better preparation and motivation for work. Too many young people do not have the hard and soft skills they need to progress in education or work. Attainment in English and Maths really matters. Too many have limited access to high-quality work experience and information and advice. The raising of the education participation age from 16 to 18 over the course of 2013–15 is a massive moment for the country. But there will only be benefits if education and training is of the right quality, in the right places, with the right incentives on schools and colleges, employers and young people.

Young people not heading for university need clear high-quality options for progression. For those young people who don't go to university, there are too few high-quality progression routes to follow as they make the transition from being in full-time education to being in full-time work. Again, the raising of the age of compulsory participation in education in England presents us with a huge opportunity to get this right. We call for more incentives on employers to engage with young people during their transition from education into work, and an expansion in the number of high-quality options available to young people (including apprenticeships). We also call for the creation of Job Ready, a locally-tailored, national programme for those most at risk of becoming long-term NEET. The programme would act early to prevent young people becoming NEET in the first place, and get those who do drop out back on track towards work rather than heading for long-term detachment from the labour market. We also propose an innovative mentoring project where young people employed for a year are automatically registered to mentor the disadvantaged to help them towards work.

Young people need reform of the welfare state, including guaranteed back-to-work support. Our analysis concludes that theories about the impact of immigration, work disincentives arising from benefit rates and an overgenerous minimum wage are largely red herrings in the debate about youth unemployment. The cost of transport is an issue for many.

Published by ACEVO in 2012

⇨ The above information is reprinted with kind permission from ACEVO. Please visit www.acevo.org.uk for further information.

Education to employment: getting Europe's youth into work

Youth unemployment across the European Union remains unacceptably high, to the detriment of current and future generations. Addressing it requires understanding its causes and then relentlessly pursuing solutions.

The problem of youth unemployment in the European Union is not new. Youth unemployment has been double or even triple the rate of general unemployment in Europe for the last 20 years. The events of the past few years have dramatically exacerbated it, however: 5.6 million young people are unemployed across Europe, and a total of 7.5 million are neither being educated nor are they working. Moreover, while young people are eager to work, more than half of those without jobs say they simply can't find one – all while businesses across Europe insist they struggle to find young people with the skills they need.

To understand this disconnect and what can be done about it, McKinsey built on the methodology used in our 2012 publication, *Education to Employment: Designing a System that Works*. We concentrated on four broad questions:

⇨ Is the scale of the youth-unemployment problem in Europe a result of lack of jobs, lack of skills, or lack of coordination?

⇨ What are the obstacles that youth face on their journey from education to employment?

⇨ Which groups of youth and employers in Europe are struggling the most?

⇨ What can be done to address the problem?

To answer these questions, we surveyed 5,300 youth, 2,600 employers, and 700 post secondary-education providers across eight countries that together are home to almost 73 per cent of Europe's 5.6 million jobless youth: France, Germany, Greece, Italy, Portugal, Spain, Sweden and the United Kingdom. We also examined more than 100 programmes in 25 countries to provide examples of companies, governments, education providers, and nongovernmental organizations that may be relevant to Europe.

Our research led us to the following answers:

While there are more people looking for work, employers in Europe cannot find the skills they need

Clearly, the lack of availability of jobs in Europe is part of the problem, but it is far from the whole story. In many countries, the number of people employed has actually remained steady, and in some countries, increased, since 2005. A greater number of older people are working longer, and more women with children are choosing to join or remain in the workforce. Across the 15 countries that were members of the EU prior to May 2004, for example, the percentage of people aged 55 to 59 who are in the labour market has jumped 11 percentage points since 2005, while increasing four percentage points among women aged 35 to 39. This increase in the participation rate in a demand-constrained environment means greater competition for jobs for younger people, who are disadvantaged by their lack of proven experience. Meanwhile, labour-market regulations that discourage hiring and firing, which are common in Europe, make it even more difficult for youth to step onto the first rung of the employment ladder.

Yet despite this availability of labour, employers are dissatisfied with applicants' skills: 27 per cent reported that they have left a vacancy open in the past year because they could not find anyone with the right skills. One-third said the lack of skills is causing major business problems, in the form of cost, quality or time. Counterintuitively, employers from countries where youth unemployment is highest reported the greatest problems. So why is it that young people are not getting the skills that employers need? One reason is the failure of employers, education providers and young people to understand one another. To cite our 2012 report, they operate in 'parallel universes'.

In Europe, 74 per cent of education providers were confident that their graduates were prepared for work, but only 38 per cent of youth and 35 per cent of employers agreed. The different players don't talk to one another and don't understand one another's expectations and needs. Only in Germany and the United Kingdom did most employers report that they communicate with education providers at least several times a year. In Portugal, only a third did. And only in Spain did most employers report that their interactions with providers were actually effective.

Youth face three significant hurdles

The education-to-employment (E2E) path can be described as a road with three intersections: enrolling in post-secondary education, building the right skills and finding a suitable job. The problem is that in Europe there are roadblocks at each of these three points.

When it comes to enrolling in further education, the most significant barrier in Europe is cost. Although university tuition fees are usually highly subsidised in Europe, many students find the cost of living while studying too high to sustain. Also, in a number of countries, non-academic, vocational courses are not subsidised and can therefore be prohibitively expensive. Students also lack information: except in Germany, less than 25 per cent said they received sufficient information on post-secondary courses and careers to guide their decisions. And finally, most of those surveyed said they perceived a social bias against vocational education; less than half of those who wanted to undertake a vocational course actually did so.

At the second intersection, young people are often not learning a sufficient portfolio of general skills while they study, with employers reporting a particular shortage of soft skills such as spoken communication and work ethic. Employers and providers are not working together closely to address this.

At the final intersection, young people find the transition to work difficult. One-third fall into interim jobs after graduating, and many more struggle to find a job at all. Many lack access to career-support services at their post-secondary institution. Many more do not pursue a work placement, in spite of this being a good predictor of how quickly a young person will find a job after his or her studies are completed.

There are proven ways to improve the E2E journey

Europe's governments, employers, education providers and families are operating in difficult circumstances, but there are ways to ease the burden on all of these groups.

Innovate with design, course delivery, and financing to make education more affordable and accessible

To reduce the cost of courses, one solution is to break up degree or vocational programmes into individual modules that focus on building a particular set of skills while still counting towards a degree or formal qualification.

Each of these modules would be short (weeks or months) and self-contained, enabling young people to combine and sequence them in the order that makes most sense for their career aspirations. This model also enables young people to take a break in their studies to work for a period, and then return and pick up where they left off.

To improve financing, governments and private financial institutions can offer low-interest loans to students pursuing courses that have a strong employment record; they can also explore initiatives that allow young people to repay loans in the form of services, such as tutoring younger students. Employers can play a role by promising jobs to young people (following a rigorous recruitment process) and then assuming responsibility for part or all of the costs of education in return for the opportunity to select the most successful graduates, trained with the most relevant skills they need. This latter option is only likely to be successful, however, for employers in sectors that face either a skills scarcity or high employee turnover.

Focus young people, employers, and education providers on improving employment readiness

Young people, employers and providers must change how they think about the E2E process. To make rational decisions, young people need to think more strategically about their futures. This is particularly important in Europe, where students often have to make life-defining decisions about their educational future by age 15 – the time when many choose whether to pursue academic or vocational tracks. Students need more and better-quality information about different career paths, and need to be motivated to use it.

Education providers should focus more on what happens to

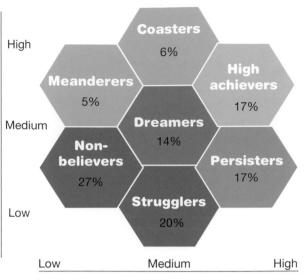

Desire for employability
How great was your desire to become employable?

students after they leave school. Specifically, they should track graduates' employment and their job satisfaction. To improve student prospects, education providers could work more closely with employers to make sure they are offering courses that really help young people prepare for the workplace.

Employers cannot wait for the right applicants to show up at their doorsteps. In the most effective interventions, employers and education providers work closely to design curricula that fit business needs; employers may even participate in teaching, by providing instructors. They might also consider increasing the availability of work placements and opportunities for practical learning. Larger enterprises may be able to go further, by setting up training academies to improve required skills for both themselves and their suppliers.

Build the supporting structures that allow the best interventions to scale up

At a national level in Europe, responsibility and oversight of the E2E highway is split across multiple government departments, resulting in a fragmented and confusing picture. One way to improve this is to create a 'system integrator' to gather and share information on the most salient metrics: job forecasts by profession, youth job-placement rates, employer satisfaction with the graduates of different programmes, and so on. The system integrator would also identify and share examples of successful programmes and work with employers and educators to create sectoral or regional solutions based on these. Technological solutions can also help to compensate for shortages of apprenticeships and other forms of short-term work placements. 'Serious games' that mimic the workplace context, for example, are low-cost, low-risk ways for students to receive a personalised learning experience through repeated 'play' of the game. While not a full substitute for an actual apprenticeship, this approach offers a substantial step forward in providing the applied skills that employers say young people lack; furthermore, such initiatives can be made available to greater numbers of young people without needing to find more employers to provide work placements.

Involve the European Union

To help the most successful interventions reach the greatest number of young people, the European Union has a critical role to play in three areas:

⇨ Information. The European Union could develop and share a more comprehensive labour-market platform incorporating the most relevant data to capture employment trends in each sector and region. This would help institutional decision makers, employers and job seekers make better decisions; for instance, by helping users understand the implications of the data – whether on the courses they should offer as an education provider or the skills gaps they should try to fill as a group of employers within an industry.

⇨ Mobility. The European Union can improve educational and labour mobility by working to make vocational qualifications transferable across borders, as has already largely been achieved in the university-education process in Bologna.

⇨ Sharing relevant practices on matching labour-market demand and supply. The European Union is in the best position to take the lead on helping national public-employment services compare their successful interventions, and then disseminate and promote those that are relevant to similar-context countries.

Youth unemployment is a profound challenge to the future of Europe, and both individual countries and the European Union recognise this. Only by reaching across their parallel universes can all parties affected by the crisis of youth unemployment create an education-to-employment system that works more effectively and benefits all.

For more on this research, download the full report, *Education to Employment: Getting Europe's Youth into Work*.

For more on the 2012 methodology on which this report builds, download *Education to Employment: Designing a System that Works*.

About the authors

Mona Mourshed is a director in McKinsey's Washington, DC, office; Jigar Patel is a principal in the London office; and Katrin Suder is a director in the Berlin office.

January 2014

⇨ The above information is reprinted with kind permission from McKinsey & Company. Please visit www.mckinsey.com for further information.

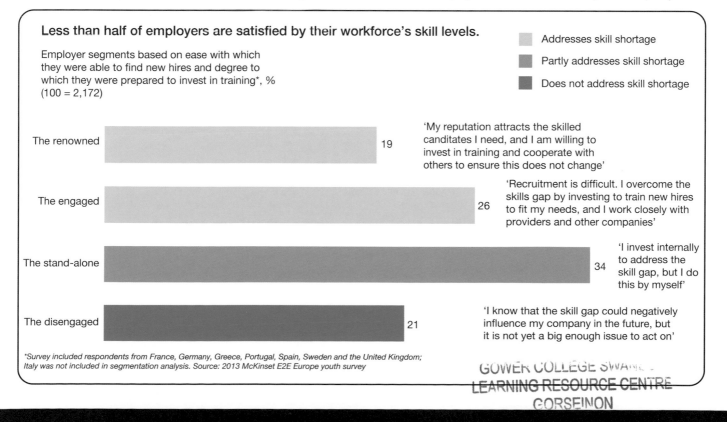

Less than half of employers are satisfied by their workforce's skill levels.

Employer segments based on ease with which they were able to find new hires and degree to which they were prepared to invest in training*, % (100 = 2,172)

Addresses skill shortage
Partly addresses skill shortage
Does not address skill shortage

The renowned — 19
'My reputation attracts the skilled candidates I need, and I am willing to invest in training and cooperate with others to ensure this does not change'

The engaged — 26
'Recruitment is difficult. I overcome the skills gap by investing to train new hires to fit my needs, and I work closely with providers and other companies'

The stand-alone — 34
'I invest internally to address the skill gap, but I do this by myself'

The disengaged — 21
'I know that the skill gap could negatively influence my company in the future, but it is not yet a big enough issue to act on'

*Survey included respondents from France, Germany, Greece, Portugal, Spain, Sweden and the United Kingdom; Italy was not included in segmentation analysis. Source: 2013 McKinset E2E Europe youth survey

New survey of final year university students shows those with work experience are three times more likely to get a graduate job offer

Major new research with over 18,000 final-year university students from the 'Class of 2013' confirms that finalists who had completed an internship or other vacation work with employers during their studies were three times more likely to receive a definite job offer before leaving university, compared with undergraduates who had done no work experience at all.

The UK Graduate Careers Survey 2013 was conducted by High Fliers Research, the independent research company that specialises in student and graduate research. The survey was based on face-to-face interviews with 18,252 final-year students from 30 key universities, completed on campus in March 2013. This sample includes a fifth of the finalists due to graduate from these universities in the summer of 2013.

The research also shows that students leaving Britain's leading universities in 2013 started looking for graduate jobs earlier than ever before and have made an unprecedented number of applications to employers. The total number of graduate job applications made by this year's university leavers is now 75% higher than five years ago.

The key findings from *The UK Graduate Careers Survey 2013* about the 'Class of 2013' are:

⇨ For the third consecutive year, the percentage of final-year students expecting to join the graduate

job market after university has increased noticeably. 44% of finalists – the highest proportion since 1998 – believed they would either start a graduate job or be looking for a graduate job after university, compared with 42% in 2012, 40% in 2011 and 36% in both 2010 and 2009.

⇨ Postgraduate study is a very popular alternative to employment, with 26% of final-year students hoping to go on to further study, but the number of students planning to take time off or go travelling after university has dropped to its lowest level ever – just 11% of finalists intend to have a break after their studies.

⇨ Final-year students' confidence in the graduate job market has improved a little, with fewer finalists describing the employment prospects for university-leavers as 'limited'.

⇨ 70% of students began researching their career options before the beginning of their final year at university, the highest-proportion ever recorded by *The UK Graduate Careers Survey*.

⇨ A total of 41% of finalists made job applications to graduate employers almost a year before graduation – applying for graduate vacancies in September or October at the very beginning of their final year at university. This compares with 37% who applied

early in 2011, 31% in 2009, 28% in 2006 and 25% in 2001.

⇨ By the time the survey took place in March, an unprecedented 63% of finalists had made graduate job applications, compared with the 61% who had applied by the same point last year, 59% in 2011 and 55% in 2010. The average number of graduate job applications made by finalists has increased too, from 5.7 applications per student in 2009–2010 and 6.9 applications per student in 2011–2012, to a record 7.1 applications per student this year.

⇨ Together, these results account for a 75% increase in the overall volume of graduate job applications, compared with five years ago. Students at the 30 universities included in the survey have made an estimated 427,000 job applications this year, compared with 360,000 in 2012, 257,000 in 2010 and 244,000 in 2008.

⇨ 36% of applicants who had done an internship or other vacation work with a graduate employer had received at least one definite job offer by March 2013, compared with just 11% of applicants who'd had no careers-related work experience whilst at university.

⇨ For the second year running, marketing is the most popular destination for new graduates, ahead of jobs in the media, consulting and teaching. Applications for the engineering jobs increased by almost 12% but fewer finalists applied for graduate positions in retailing, investment banking and the Armed Forces.

⇨ The average expected starting salary for new graduates has increased a little to £22,800, the first time that salary expectations have overtaken those anticipated in 2008. After five years in work, today's graduates expect to be earning an average of £40,400 and a sixth of finalists believe their salary will be £100,000 or more by the age of 30.

⇨ London is again the preferred employment destination for finalists and 50% of student job hunters hoped to work in the capital after graduation – the highest proportion ever recorded by the survey. London remains the first choice at 27 out of the 30 universities included in the survey but finalists at Queen's University Belfast, Glasgow and Strathclyde planned to work close to where they'd been studying, upon completion of their degrees.

⇨ Two-thirds of students who left their graduate job search until the final year at university said they'd realised they should have started job hunting earlier.

Managing director of High Fliers Research, Martin Birchall commented:

'Our latest research highlights that work experience is no longer an optional extra for university students, it's an essential part of preparing for the graduate job market. Students who just focus on their degree studies without spending time in the workplace are unlikely to develop the skills and interests that graduate employers are looking for.

'The survey also shows just how hard today's university students are working to secure a graduate job at the end of their degree. Record numbers of students are now choosing to research their career options in their first or second year at university, rather than leaving job hunting until the final six months before graduation.'

13 June 2013

⇨ The above information is reprinted with kind permission from High Fliers Research. Please visit www.highfliers.co.uk for further information.

© *High Fliers Research*

Learning to work: survey report

Today's young people, tomorrow's workforce.

Recruiting young people

One in four employers did not recruit a single young person aged 16–24 in the last 12 months, rising to three in ten organisations in the private and voluntary sectors. Public sector organisations are most likely to have recruited young people over the last year, with 74% saying this is the case.

The number one reason employers recruited young people is that they want to grow their own workforce, with 40% of employers that recruited young people saying this is the case, while more than a third of respondents (38%) cite wanting to build their own talent pipeline.

Looking ahead, just 56% of employers report they are likely to recruit young people within the next 12 months. In all, 58% of private sector employers say they are likely to recruit young people over the next year, as do 52% of public sector organisations and 46% of voluntary sector employers.

The main reasons that would encourage employers to recruit young people are more job vacancies arising in their organisation, for example as a result of people leaving and the creation of new vacancies through increased demand for products and services.

However, almost a quarter of employers say that an increase in the quality of applications from young people would encourage them to recruit them and a similar proportion cite help with funding from the Government.

A further 22% report that greater assurance that the education system is delivering more job-ready young people would encourage them to recruit from this age cohort.

Employers' perceptions of young people

The survey asked respondents to agree or disagree with a series of statements to gauge their overall attitude to young people in the labour market. Nearly half of employers (47%) agree that young people are disadvantaged in today's labour market. They also believe that young people need an opportunity to prove themselves, with 64% agreeing or strongly agreeing that this is the case.

Some employers express concerns about young people's readiness for work, with 59% agreeing they have unrealistic expectations about work, and 63% agreeing they lack insight into the working world. In all, 57% of respondents agree young people lack work experience and 53% think they lack adequate career guidance. Almost half of respondents say young people are not prepared for work.

However, among HR (Human Resources) professionals that have recruited young people in the last 12 months, satisfaction levels are generally high. In all, 91% of employers are either very satisfied (26%) or fairly satisfied (65%) with the young people they have recruited. Just 9% of respondents report they are fairly or very dissatisfied.

There is little sector variation, with high levels of satisfaction across the private, public and voluntary sectors.

The business case for employing young people

Almost three-quarters (74%) of employers think there is a business case for employing young people. In all, just 10% disagree and 17% don't know.

Among employers that believe there is a business case for employing young people, the most commonly cited reason is that they demonstrate a willingness to learn, with private sector employers particularly highlighting this as a benefit.

More than four in ten organisations highlight the ability of young people to bring in fresh ideas and new approaches as a business benefit. In all, 53% of voluntary sector respondents identify this as an attribute that young people bring to the business, as do 43% of private

- WHERE'S YOUR **WORK** EXPERIENCE?

- EMPLOY US AND YOU'LL SEE!!

JOB READY

JOB

sector employers and 40% of those in the public sector.

A similar proportion of employers (42%) report that young people bring in motivation, energy and optimism, with 44% of public sector and voluntary sector respondents identifying this as a benefit that young people bring to the business, and 40% of those in the private sector.

More than a quarter of respondents identify both cost-effectiveness and improving workforce diversity as part of the business case for employing young people.

There is a strong link between employers that believe there is a business case for employing young people and those that have recruited young people in the last 12 months. Almost three-quarters (72%) of employers that agree there is a business case have recruited young people in the last 12 months compared with just 54% that are not convinced by the business case for employing young people.

The role of employers in engaging with young people and education

Seven out of ten respondents believe employers have a duty to help tackle youth employment, with 18% disagreeing and 11% saying they don't know. Voluntary sector employers are most likely to think employers have a role to play (81%).

Giving young people early exposure to the workplace through initiatives such as work experience and internship placements is most commonly viewed by employers as being part of their role in helping young people and tackling youth employment. Three-quarters of employers (76%) cite this as being a way that they can help young people.

Nearly two-thirds (61%) of employers think they can help young people by providing career insights in the classroom through school visits and talks to schoolchildren.

More than half of respondents (56%) think employers can help young people into employment by providing them with insights into recruitment, such as mock interviews and help with writing CVs.

The survey highlights a significant gap between the ways in which respondents believe employers can help young people and what is happening on the ground. Just 41% of respondents say their organisation provides access routes into their organisation for non-graduates.

Six in ten employers provide work experience placements, and about a quarter of respondents (24%) say their organisation offers internships.

The majority of employers believe they should become more involved in education in order to help young people. Almost seven in ten respondents believe that employers should have either a little (45%) or a lot more involvement (23%) with education.

There is a clear correlation between employers that are already engaging with young people through links with schools and colleges and those that are intending to recruit young people in the next year.

For example, almost 73% of employers that provide access routes into the organisation for non-graduates are planning to recruit young people in the next year, compared with a survey average of 56%.

September 2012

⇨ The above information is reprinted with kind permission from CIPD. Please visit www.cipd.co.uk for further information.

Results from the *Annual Survey of Hours and Earnings, 2013* (provisional results)
Office for National Statistics, 12 December 2013

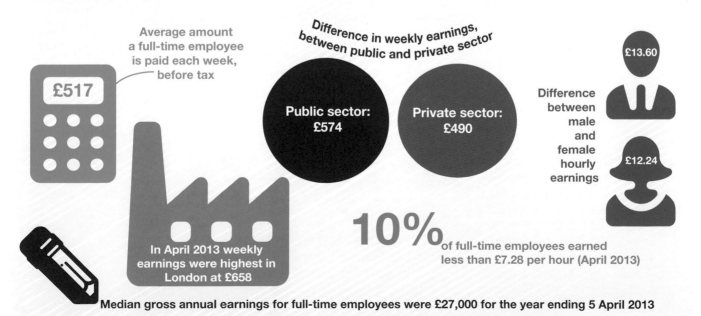

Average amount a full-time employee is paid each week, before tax

£517

In April 2013 weekly earnings were highest in London at £658

Difference in weekly earnings, between public and private sector

Public sector: £574

Private sector: £490

10% of full-time employees earned less than £7.28 per hour (April 2013)

£13.60

Difference between male and female hourly earnings

£12.24

Median gross annual earnings for full-time employees were £27,000 for the year ending 5 April 2013

Should enterprise education be introduced to the National Curriculum?

Enterprise Nation editor Simon Wickes takes a look at our most recent poll result and considers whether there's real value in teaching enterprise in schools.

We asked Enterprise Nation readers the question: Should enterprise education be introduced to the National Curriculum? writes Simon Wickes. 90 per cent of more than 200 voters said 'Yes'. Clearly – among businesses, at least, there's a strong appetite to see business skills and entrepreneurship become a part of every child's education – or at least a developed option that could perhaps be run as an optional GCSE or A-level.

But how practical is it to make enterprise a National Curriculum subject? Is there any evidence that learning about enterprise at school actually increases the desire among young people to start their own business; or that it encourages them to take a more entrepreneurial attitude into the world of employment?

Is it feasible to make enterprise education part of the National Curriculum?

At present, enterprise education is recommended, rather than required. Successive governments have promoted the idea of teaching business skills to young people and the increasing number of schools being turned into specialist academies opens the door for greater involvement of business in education. On top of this, there are a large number of organisations that work with schools on enterprise initiatives, such as enterprise days and extra-curricular activities for pupils. However, enterprise education remains a largely voluntary activity, the practice of which is dependent on the choices made by individual schools and their commitment to carrying it out. The 2010 publication *A Guide to Enterprise Education* from the now defunct Department for Children, Schools and Families outlines how schools can integrate enterprise into the existing curriculum across subjects and deals with issues of teacher training, developing an enterprise culture within the school, and so on. Critically, the report states that:

'If enterprise is delivered as a standalone subject or a separate activity, it will be more time consuming and less effective than if it is integrated into the existing curriculum... Their [enterprise co-ordinators'] approach has been to encourage colleagues across their school to integrate enterprise into their own lesson plans and approaches.'

The report provokes a number of questions about the delivery of enterprise education:

⇨ Would a standalone enterprise curriculum actually be more effective than introducing enterprise angles to existing subjects within the curriculum as it stands?

In the latter case, how do you ensure teachers have the knowledge and confidence to introduce ideas of enterprise into their subject area?

⇨ How are teachers even going to find the time to introduce a fresh set of ideas to their subject?

We might also ask: What would you teach under the heading of enterprise education anyway, and is there enough to say or do to cover a two-year curriculum?

Enterprise education: does it actually make students more entrepreneurial?

Of course, there's another enormous question:

⇨ Does enterprise education actually increase pupils' employability or their desire to start their own business? Can it unlock the innate entrepreneurialism within our young people?

⇨ A June 2013 report from the Department of Business Innovation and Skills, *Enterprise Education Impact on Higher Education and Further Education*, suggests that the effect of the existing delivery of enterprise education is variable:

'While the evidence suggests that enterprise and entrepreneurship education generally has positive benefits that should be expected to lead to some students starting new businesses and making contributions to the growth of existing businesses, for example, the evidence does not conclusively show the attribution of this to enterprise and entrepreneurship education in either FE or HE.'

It's a bit garbled, but the report seems to be saying that the evidence suggests that students who receive some form of enterprise education *do* pick up useful business skills, *do* acquire a more entrepreneurial outlook and *are* more likely to think about starting their own business. The evidence relating to whether they will *actually* do so, however, is mixed: some studies suggest there's no distinct relationship between enterprise education and subsequent entrepreneurialism; other studies suggest there is such a relationship. But it's all a bit inconclusive and the report's authors are reluctant to stick their necks out. We know at Enterprise Nation that current owners of start-ups and micro-businesses are hungry for knowledge that would help them run their business more effectively. There's no doubt that enterprise education would have had considerable value for these people and might even have prompted them to become self-employed at an earlier stage. Whether it should be a National Curriculum subject is another matter, though – and there's plenty of debate to be had there about what exactly to teach and how best to deliver it.

What can you do to get involved in enterprise education?

Laura Hampton of Hallam Internet has today written about one example of a business-owner supporting enterprise education at a summer school, and the benefits of doing so. The 2010 Guide mentioned above contains a number of other suggestions for what businesses can do if they build a relationship with local schools. So if you're interested in supporting the next generation of small business-owners, it's well worth contacting your local schools to find out what they do in terms of teaching enterprise. There are also a number of external delivery organisations you could approach. In fact, there are loads of people already doing this, often in very inventive ways. Here are a few that work with businesses:

⇨ Education Business Partnerships – find your local EBP on the IEBE website

⇨ Young Enterprise

⇨ Make Your Mark

⇨ Prince's Trust

⇨ Young Chamber

⇨ Industrial Trust

⇨ Enterprise Education Trust

⇨ Business in the Community

⇨ Bright Futures

⇨ IEBE.

You'll find plenty of others, too, if you do a little research.

11 July 2013

⇨ The above information is reprinted with kind permission from Enterprise Nation. Please visit www.enterprisenation.com for further information.

Jobseeking made tougher by 'false jobs'

Why do organisations advertise jobs if the position has already been filled? Here, one young jobseeker discusses his frustrations with 'false jobs'.

These last 18 months I have had the misfortune of being one of the many young unemployed citizens of Great Britain. In this time I have sent off hundreds upon hundreds of CVs, mainly using one of the many job sites which advertise thousands of jobs for companies who are seemingly willing to pay large advertising fees in order to get the right employee.

So why am I not employed yet? Or why, for that matter, do I rarely even receive a reply back? Is my CV really that bad? Do I lack the qualifications? Are they swamped with applications? Did I insult their mother? One possible reason is that some of these positions are filled even before they're advertised on these job sites, either by internal promotion or by friends and family of other employees at the company.

Getting a job through a friend or family member has always been the easiest and most reliable way of finding work; after all, employers are far more likely to employ someone they know or someone who has been recommended to them than some stranger who sent their details by email. Picking someone they've known for more than an hour during an interview gives them peace of mind and also saves them money, since they no longer have to advertise the job.

But wait a minute … If that's the case then why am I looking at an advert for that same job in my local paper? The problem is some employers are required to advertise externally and consider all candidates, even if their mind is already made up and all the applications will be going straight in the bin. In the last place I worked, jobs were advertised internally a week before they were advertised externally, giving us plenty of time to apply for the position and talk with the team and manager in order to assure them we were the right man or woman for the job.

The issue here isn't so much with employers already having a job filled before it's advertised but with the fact it's advertised at all. When I go to a jobsite and apply for ten jobs, I want to come away knowing that someone will look at those CVs and take them into consideration, and the only way to assure this would be if laws and policies that require these jobs to be advertised were changed or removed. Only employers who were genuinely interested in looking for new employees would then be advertising vacancies, cutting out the many 'false' jobs and allowing unemployed people such as myself to apply with the confidence that we will be noticed.

Is that likely to happen? Who knows? To be honest there isn't much I or any other jobseekers can do to change the rules about advertising. There is, however, something those looking for work can do to avoid their CVs being binned as soon as they apply and that is to apply before any job is even advertised. Send your CV off to a company with a covering letter simply describing the fact that you're looking for work, outlining your skills and explaining why you'd be a great addition to that company. By using your initiative, you can get ahead of the pack and if you make a good impression you may just land yourself a job.

2012

⇨ The above information is reprinted with kind permission from Headliners. Please visit www.headliners.org for further information.

Sherlock Holmes Museum curator scorns 'lazy' job applicant for vacancy enquiry

The curator of the Sherlock Holmes Museum has sparked outrage on social media by suggesting job applicant Rachel Fox was 'lazy' and 'selfish' for requesting more details about a vacancy.

Fox posted the response from museum creator Andrea von Ehrenstein, writing: 'After enquiring about a job vacancy they had listed and requesting further details I am told I am lazy and selfish.'

Ehrenstein told the job applicant: 'You have to think first whether we might want to answer all your questions even supposing we had the time.'

'The first thing is to send your CV to an employer and then ask questions if the employer is at all interested in you. You are putting yourself first in life instead of thinking about what the other person might want from you.

'We are not interested in a series of questions from a person who cannot be bothered to include their own CV in their enquiry. It sounds very much like you are simply working for a recruitment agency.'

On trying to reply to Ehrenstein's message, Fox wrote that she was left 'speechless' to discover that her email had been 'blocked and reported as spam'.

Twitter users flocked to her defence, with Matt Wilcox writing that the museum creator was 'doing an excellent job of damaging their own business ... by being lazy and selfish!'.

Another user, Betsy, said the curator's response was 'shockingly bad. She added: 'And "yours sincerely" is making me laugh when an offer to "assist further" is anything but.'

Fox originally wrote to the Museum, which is at the famous detective's address of 221b Baker Street in London, asking for more details about a retail staff post and for a 'slightly more detailed job specification'.

The fine arts graduate from Nottingham Trent University later wrote that the response she got was 'so rude' and quipped: 'If anything, I totally dodged a bullet with that one. Glad to not work there!'

Patrick Woodman, head of external affairs at the Chartered Management Institute, told *HuffPostUK*: 'This isn't the first time that a manager has been wrong-footed by the power of social media – just remember when the energy companies announced price rises recently – and it won't be the last.

'In fact, CMI's research shows that two-thirds of today's managers today admit they don't know how to use social media effectively. New technology creates brilliant opportunities, but this story is a reminder that reputations can be badly damaged in the blink of an eye.'

17 February 2014

⇨ The above information is reprinted with kind permission from *Huffington Post UK*. Please visit www.huffingtonpost.co.uk for further information.

© 2014 AOL (UK) Limited

Who do you agree with?

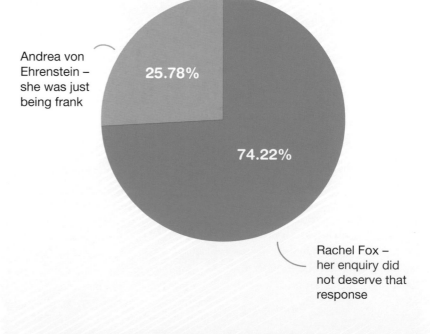

Andrea von Ehrenstein – she was just being frank 25.78%

Rachel Fox – her enquiry did not deserve that response 74.22%

Job insecurity or job reorganisation thought to be the most common cause of work-related stress

⇨ Half of workers across Europe think work-related stress is common, and four in ten think it is not handled well at their workplace.

⇨ Job insecurity or job reorganisation is thought to be the most common cause of work-related stress across Europe.

⇨ There is low awareness of programmes or policies to make it easier for workers to continue working up to or beyond the retirement age, though the majority support their introduction.

These are the main findings of the third edition of the pan-European opinion poll conducted by Ipsos MORI on behalf of the European Agency for Safety and Health at Work (EU-OSHA).

Work-related stress

Around half of workers across Europe (51%) perceive that work-related stress is common in their workplace, with 16% saying it is 'very common' according to the poll. Female workers are more likely than male workers to say that work-related stress is common (54% vs 49%), as are workers aged 18–54 (53%) compared with workers aged 55+ (44%). Perceptions of work-related stress also vary by sector with those in health or care work being the most likely to say cases of work-related stress are common (61% including 21% who say cases are 'very common').

There is a link between the proportion of workers who say work-related stress is common where they work and those workers who say that work-related stress is not controlled well. Seven in ten (72%) workers across Europe who say work-related stress is rare in their workplace also say it is controlled well, while conversely six in ten (58%) workers who say work-related stress is common where they work also believe that it is not controlled well.

The most common cause of work-related stress across Europe is perceived to be job insecurity or job reorganisation (72%) followed by hours worked or workload (66%). However, among younger workers aged 18–34, these two causes are ranked joint highest (both at 69%). Furthermore, health or care workers are much more likely than average to select hours worked/workload (77%).

In countries with a higher level of public debt, workers are more likely to cite job insecurity or job reorganisation as a perceived cause of work-related stress; 73% of workers in countries with public debt of more than 90% of GDP choose job insecurity or job reorganisation as a common cause work-related stress compared to 66% of those in countries with public debt of 60% of GDP or less.[1]

Unacceptable behaviours such as bullying or harassment are perceived as a common cause of work-related stress by six in ten workers (59%). Fewer workers perceive a lack of support from colleagues or superiors (57%), a lack of clarity on roles and responsibilities (52%) or limited opportunity to manage work patterns (46%) as common causes of work-related stress.

Active ageing

Across Europe, half of those polled (52%) expect the proportion of workers aged 60+ in their workplace to increase by 2020 (43% think this is unlikely). Workers aged 55+ are more likely to think there will be a higher proportion of people aged 60+ in their workplace in 2020 (59%) than those aged 35–54 (54%), and younger workers aged 18–34 (45%).

One in eight workers (12%) are aware of policies and programmes making it easier for older workers to continue working up to or beyond retirement age. Awareness of policies increases as workplace size increases from 7% in the smallest workplaces (one to ten workers) up to 19% in the largest workplaces (more than 250 workers). Among those who are not aware of such programmes and policies, 61% support their introduction. Groups more likely to favour these policies include women, part-time workers, health or care workers and those in larger workplaces. Older workers aged 55+ are only slightly more likely than younger workers to support such policies (64% vs 61% of workers aged 35–54 and 60% of workers aged 18–34.

When asked whether they thought older workers aged 60+ were more prone to certain behaviours than other workers:

⇨ Only two in ten workers (22%) perceive older workers to have more accidents at work than other workers (this relationship is consistent among most groups although manual workers are slightly more likely to think this);

⇨ Around three in ten (28%) think that older workers aged 60+ are less productive at work than other workers;

⇨ Four in ten (42%) think that older workers tend to suffer more from work-related stress than other workers, while slightly more workers think the converse (48%); and

⇨ Six in ten workers (60%) believe that workers aged 60+ are less likely to be able to adapt to changes at work than other workers, and this perception is held by half (49%) of older workers aged 55+ (though it should be noted one in three of all workers (33%) believe that it is other workers who are less able to adapt to changes at work).

Note:

1: Public debt as a % of GDP data is from Eurostat, 2012 Q2. Countries with public debt at more than 90% of GDP are Greece, Italy, Belgium,

Ireland, Portugal, France and Iceland. Countries with public debt at 60% or less of GDP are Poland, Finland, Latvia, Denmark, Slovakia, Sweden, Czech Republic, Lithuania, Slovenia, Romania, Luxembourg, Bulgaria, Estonia, Switzerland, Liechtenstein and Norway.

9 May 2013

⇨ The above information is reprinted with kind permission from Ipsos MORI. Please visit www.ipsos. co.uk for further information.

Majority of workers burned out at work

As unemployed workers contend with a highly competitive job market, the post-recession workplace norm of smaller staffs, longer hours and increased workloads is taking its toll on those currently employed. 74% of British workers say they feel burned out in their current job with more than one-in-ten stating they feel burned out all the time. The infographic below summarises this survey.

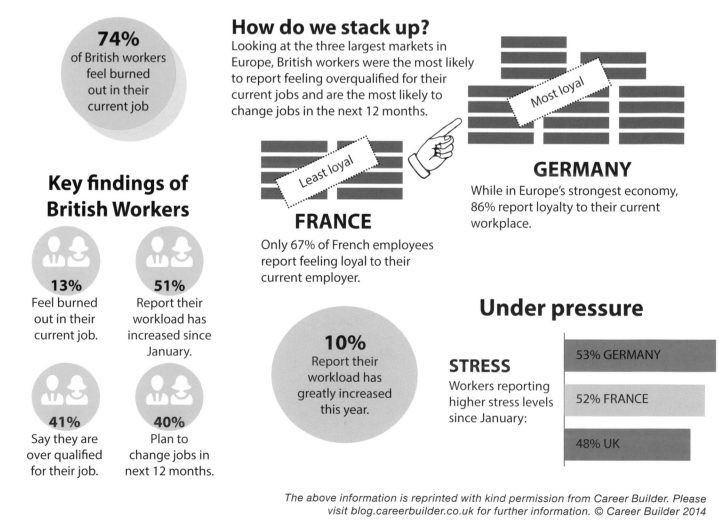

74% of British workers feel burned out in their current job

Key findings of British Workers

13% Feel burned out in their current job.

51% Report their workload has increased since January.

41% Say they are over qualified for their job.

40% Plan to change jobs in next 12 months.

How do we stack up?

Looking at the three largest markets in Europe, British workers were the most likely to report feeling overqualified for their current jobs and are the most likely to change jobs in the next 12 months.

Least loyal

Most loyal

FRANCE

Only 67% of French employees report feeling loyal to their current employer.

GERMANY

While in Europe's strongest economy, 86% report loyalty to their current workplace.

10% Report their workload has greatly increased this year.

Under pressure

STRESS
Workers reporting higher stress levels since January:

53% GERMANY

52% FRANCE

48% UK

The above information is reprinted with kind permission from Career Builder. Please visit blog.careerbuilder.co.uk for further information. © Career Builder 2014

Flexible working

1. Overview

Flexible working is a way of working that suits an employee's needs, e.g. being able to work certain hours or work from home.

Anyone can ask their employer to work flexibly.

Employees who care for someone (e.g. a child or adult) have the legal right to ask for flexible working.

This is also known as 'making a statutory application'. However, you have to qualify and your employer doesn't have to agree to the request.

2. Types of flexible working

There are different ways of working flexibly.

Job sharing

Two people do one job and split the hours.

Working from home

It might be possible to do some or all of the work from home or anywhere else other than the normal place of work.

Part time

Working less than full-time hours (usually by working fewer days).

Compressed hours

Working full-time hours but over fewer days.

Flexitime

The employee chooses when to start and end work (within agreed limits) but works certain 'core hours', e.g. 10am to 4pm every day.

Annualised hours

The employee has to work a certain number of hours over the year but they have some flexibility about when they work. There are sometimes 'core hours' which the employee regularly works each week, and they work the rest of their hours flexibly or when there's extra demand at work.

Staggered hours

The employee has different start, finish and break times from other workers.

Phased retirement

Default retirement age has been phased out and older workers can choose when they want to retire. This means they can reduce their hours and work part time.

3. Making a statutory application

The basic steps for making an application are:

⇨ The employee writes to the employer.

⇨ The employer should request a meeting within 28 days to discuss the application.

⇨ The employer must make a decision within 14 days of the meeting and tell the employee about it.

⇨ If the employer agrees to flexible working they must give the employee a new contract. If they don't agree the employee can appeal.

Employees can only make a statutory application if they have worked continuously for the same employer for the last 26 weeks.

Employees can only make one statutory application each year.

Writing to the employer

Employees can write their own email or letter to their employer, or use a template.

Employers can also ask the employee to use a standard form to make an application.

What the letter must include

All applications must be in writing.

The application must:

⇨ be dated

⇨ say that the employee either has responsibility as a parent or carer (or expects to have it)

↳ say that they're making the application under the statutory right to request a flexible working pattern

- give details about how they want to work flexibly and when they want to start

- explain how they think flexible working might affect the business and how this could be dealt with (e.g. if they're not at work on certain days)

- say if and when they've made a previous application.

The employee doesn't have to include proof that:

- they're a parent or carer

- no-one else can care for the child or adult they're responsible for.

Meeting to discuss the application

The meeting must happen within 28 days of the employer receiving the application.

If the responsible manager isn't at work, the 28 days start when they get back.

The employee must give a reasonable explanation if they can't attend the meeting. Otherwise the employer can treat the application as withdrawn.

Bringing someone to the meeting

Employees can bring a work colleague or trade union representative ('rep') to the meeting. The rep can discuss things with the employer but they can't answer questions on behalf of the employee.

If the colleague or rep can't make the meeting, it should be rearranged to take place within seven days. The employer must allow the work colleague paid time off to attend.

Withdrawing an application

Employees should tell the employer in writing as soon as possible. The application will be treated as withdrawn if the employee misses two meetings (without good reason) with the employer.

If the employee doesn't provide the extra information that the employer needs to make a decision, the application might be treated as withdrawn.

If the application is withdrawn, the employee can't make another one for 12 months.

4. After the application

The employer must write to the employee within 14 days of the meeting to let them know what the decision is. This time limit can be longer if they both agree.

Agreeing the application

If the employer agrees, they should give the employee a new contract. The employer should write to the employee within 28 days about this and the date the flexible working will start.

Rejecting an application

The employer's letter must include:

- the business reasons for rejecting the application

- an explanation about how flexible working affects their business

- how the employee can appeal.

Employers can only reject an application for one of the following reasons:

- extra costs which will damage the business

- the business won't be able to meet customer demand

- the work can't be reorganised among other staff

- people can't be recruited to do the work

- flexible working will have an effect on quality and performance

- there's a lack of work to do during the proposed working times

- the business is planning changes to the workforce.

If the employer doesn't agree to the request, they must have a meeting with the employee to discuss the reasons.

- The above information is reprinted with kind permission from GOV.UK. Please visit www.gov.uk for further information on this and other topics.

Why are we so obsessed with 'hard work'?

The UK has the longest average annual working hours of all the major economies in Europe, but it is far from the strongest.

Countries such as Germany, Belgium and The Netherlands have demonstrated that it is possible to have significantly shorter average hours, and have arguably fared better during economic recession. People living in countries with shorter average working hours also tend to report higher levels of life satisfaction and lower levels of stress, with the 'ideal' working week lying somewhere between 25 and 30 hours, according to the results of a recent Europe-wide survey.

Many have commented on the persistent use of the phrase 'hardworking' and especially 'hard-working families' in British politics. This week I enjoyed reading Alex Andreou's discussion of the 'mythic' hardworker. Poking fun, Andreou, who runs Sturdy Beggars Theatre Company, describes how it feels to admit, 'to myself and to the world: I am not naturally hardworking. (Cue hissing from the crowd, ladies fainting, shouts of "monster".)'

Look more closely at the image of heroic hardworkers: holding down more than one low-income job and working anti-social hours so they can support their families who they barely have the time to see in the context of rising living costs and stagnating wages, and it begins to look a lot like exploitation.

Look further up the income scale and hardwork takes on a different meaning. Even in recession, for those on higher incomes working hard has a lot to do with consumption and status. Working – as Tim Jackson, Professor of Sustainable Development at the University of Surrey, has said – 'to spend money we don't have on things we don't need to create impressions that won't last on people we don't care about'. Or, put another way, 'working long hours to earn money to buy stuff that's made and used in ways that inflict profound and irreversible damage on the ecosystem on which all life depends.'

This all begs the question, where are we running and why are we running there so fast?

Last week at Waterstone's Economists' Bookshop, nef launched a new collection of essays by leading experts in social, economic and environmental sciences, exploring that question. The book, *Time on Our Side*, points to a central dilemma: we have an economy that is damned if it grows (because of the likely negative impact on climate change) and damned if it doesn't (because of the likely impact on jobs and income).

The book argues that the simplest way of getting out of the trap is to move to a shorter working week. Since countries in the rich world seem increasingly unable to grow their economies while also reducing greenhouse gas emissions to sustainable levels, they should start facing up to a future with little or no economic growth.

One of the worst effects of a flat-lining economy is usually high unemployment – but this can be offset, to an extent, if people work fewer hours. This would mean relinquishing our 'fetish for labour productivity' and focusing on the quality of work itself: 'if there's less work to be had in the economy, for whatever reason, then perhaps we should all just work less and enjoy it'. The book suggests that instead of endeavouring to increase our salaries year on year, we could be looking to increase the amount of time we have each week to call our own.

There are obvious equity issues to be considered. Who should reduce their working hours first? What about people who are time poor because of their caring responsibilities rather than their work? A shorter working week has the potential to increase gender and income equality by redistributing paid and unpaid time, but 'flexible working' policies can also give the advantage to employers and lead to zero hours contracts over which workers have little or no control.

A shorter working week would also have to be established alongside measures to tackle low wages, to ensure that everyone could benefit from the new wealth of time. The book addresses such issues head on, cautioning that social justice, environmental sustainability and a flourishing economy are possible consequences of a shorter working week, but not inevitable. It all depends on how it's done, and the ways in which this growing body of knowledge is used to inspire practical action for a more balanced, sustainable and equitable future.

I will be discussing working time and the questions it raises for a new economy based on social justice and environmental sustainability at the Compass Conference Change: HOW? on the 30 November 2013 – I hope to see you there!

Time on Our Side: Why we all need a shorter working week, edited by Anna Coote and Jane Franklin and published by nef, is out now.

21 November 2013

⇨ The above information is reprinted with kind permission from nef. Please visit www.neweconomics.org for further information.

'I burned out from work stress'

Today, Liz Tucker is a health and well-being counsellor specialising in stress management. 14 years ago, at the age of 30, she burned out from work-related stress.

'I had a building company at the time and was working incredibly hard. It wasn't unusual for me to drive from Taunton, up to York and down to Norfolk in the space of 24 hours. I'd start work at 7am and often wouldn't finish until 8pm the following day, 36 hours later. The year I burned out, I drove over 100,000 miles.

'I loved the buzz of it. There was a lot of stress involved, but I really enjoyed the adrenaline kick of having something turn out right in the end. It was very satisfying.

'At first the work was manageable. Then, during the year before I became ill, I started working at weekends. I had no social life at all, which didn't bother me at the time.

'Then I met my partner and, because of the pressures of trying to see him and keep on top of the work, it all began to fall apart. I started feeling really tired and very lethargic. One Sunday night I went to bed early because I felt like I was getting a bit of a cold.

'When I woke on Monday, I simply couldn't get out of bed. I could move my fingers, head and feet, but I had no energy in my arms and legs.

'When the doctor told me I'd burned myself out from too much stress, I found it difficult to believe. To me, stress meant being unhappy, whereas I was really enjoying my life. But it was true: there was no work-life balance and I was living a high-stress life.

'In addition, my diet was appalling. I lived on food that I bought in petrol stations, and I hadn't been getting nearly enough sleep. My body had shut itself down in protest.

'For the next three months, I couldn't get out of bed. All I did was sleep. Very slowly, I began to improve but then, after a few months, the doctor diagnosed ME. I was housebound.

'The physical symptoms were bad but the mental "fog" was awful. It was like someone had drilled a hole in my head and filled it with concrete.

'I was like this for four years, and I was declining. My partner was beginning to wonder whether I was going to die, and when he asked the doctor, the answer was, "I simply don't know. She has the body of an 80-year-old." It was very shocking to hear.

'I think, up until that point, I'd believed the doctors knew what was right for me. So hearing that they didn't know what to do made me start thinking about my own future. With my partner, I began thinking about what was right for me to do.

'I decided I needed some pleasure in life. I had been so worried for so long. I began having a weekly massage and hypnotherapy to help me relax. I also decided not to watch anything on TV that was violent or miserable.

'The biggest turning point was when I began to pace myself. Up until then, I'd compare myself to how I was before. If I was feeling a bit better, I would try to do lots of things and then feel ill with exhaustion again. I began to realise I was setting myself unrealistic goals so I decided to take things gradually.

'After I'd started this regime of proper relaxing, it was remarkable how quickly I began to feel better. I was eating a healthy diet with lots of fruit and vegetables and I'd stopped having caffeine and alcohol. I began to notice the changes within a few weeks.

'After three months, I was feeling so much better, but because I'd spent so much time in bed, I was very weak physically.

'After six months, I was back to normal. I had lots of energy, my skin was better and I didn't have to stay in bed the whole time. It was amazing.

'I've now been working as a health and well-being counsellor for ten years. I went back to university and studied human health and biology, really just to find out what had happened to me. I found it so interesting it has turned into my career.

'I'm working really hard again and get a lot of satisfaction out of it, but the difference is that now I have a work – life balance and know what to do when things get too stressful.'

11 April 2013

⇨ The above information is reprinted with kind permission from NHS Choices. Please visit www.nhs.uk for further information.

We ask the experts: are we working too hard?

Three Cambridge University researchers answer questions about the ways in which we work.

With rising competition for jobs, and increasing pressure to excel in the workplace, a healthy work–life balance is hard to achieve. The technology we invented to make our lives run smoother means that we seldom switch off. Could we do things differently?

Our work (or lack of it) defines us. Many people with jobs spend more time with their work colleagues than with their families. Employment offers us the means to enjoy life outside work but it also constrains us, eating into our time and energy. As austerity bites deeper, competition for jobs has risen to epic proportions: there is currently an average of 18 applicants for every job in the UK (Totaljobs.com), and an average of 85 applications for graduate positions (Association of Graduate Recruiters). The pressure to succeed in the workplace has resulted in a culture of long hours that doesn't always add to productivity and inevitably damages family life. At Cambridge University, work-related topics are studied from a range of perspectives – from economics to philosophy, sociology to people management.

We asked three Cambridge University researchers to answer questions about the ways in which we work. Dr Brendan Burchell is a Reader in the Department of Sociology. His interests include the effects of labour market experiences on psychological well-being and the social psychological effects of precarious employment and unemployment. Lorna Finlayson is a Junior Research Fellow in Philosophy at King's College. She works on political philosophy and its relationship to politics, with a particular interest in theories of ideology. Dr Jochen Menges is a Lecturer at Judge Business School with extensive experience in Europe and the US. His work looks at leadership, human resource management and emotions in organisations.

How would you define 'working too hard' and why do we do it?

Brendan Burchell We can measure how hard people work in two ways: first, how many hours they work per week, and second, how much effort they put into each hour of work, or how much time pressure they are under. Usually by work we mean 'paid work' but this overlooks the amount of unpaid work people do, such as cooking, caring and cleaning in the household. Men do more paid work per week, on average, than women, but if we include unpaid work, then even women in part-time employment do more work per week on average than men in full-time employment.

Working hard and working long hours is associated with poorer health and burn-out. It is also bad for families, as parents who finish a working day late or exhausted have less time and energy for their partners and children.

Thankfully the number of hours per week that we work has been reducing considerably in the UK over the past 100 years. The amount of effort we put into each hour has been increasing over the past 25 years, but has levelled off in the past 15 years. It's difficult to pin-point the reasons for this increase in pressure at work, but likely causes are the demise of trade unions, more efficient management, greater global competition and possibly that people enjoy their jobs more, so they work harder even when there is no economic compulsion to do so.

In the UK, we have more part-time employees than most EU countries, but unfortunately we still have a high proportion of full-time male employees working long hours. One negative effect of this is to make it more difficult for women to climb to the highest status and best-paid jobs. They have to compete with men who are working long hours, which is difficult to do against the backdrop of a society where women typically bear a far greater share of domestic work than men.

Lorna Finlayson Working too hard means working harder than is good for us – and for the others around us. So what it means depends on what 'good for' means. I find it easier to know what that doesn't mean than to know what it does mean: it doesn't just mean, for instance, 'enhancing our physical fitness' or 'maximising our lifespans'. Many of the things that make our lives bearable are 'unhealthy'. In most cases, we work too hard because society compels us to do so, through creating the necessity for money, and then withholding it unless we work too hard. In the other cases, it is most probably a means of self-distraction.

Jochen Menges Working too hard means that people put too much effort into their work, day after day, month after month, without opportunities to reflect and to recharge their energy. In my study of *The Acceleration Trap* (published in Harvard Business Review) I identify three patterns of working

too hard. Some people simply try to do too much in the time they have – that is 'overloading'. Others lack focus and try to do too many different things simultaneously ('multiloading'). People deprived of any hope of retreat and feeling imprisoned by the debilitating frenzy of their workplace encounter something I describe as 'perpetual loading'. Note that working hard can be enjoyable, but working too hard is unsustainable; it saps energy, impairs people cognitively and, ironically, leads to decrements in performance in the long run.

How is increasing use of IT changing the way we work?

BB A generation ago computers were unreliable, and we were poorly trained to use them, so they probably made life a misery for lots of employees. Now the effects are probably more mixed, making jobs for some people more enjoyable by minimising the repetitive and boring components of work, but making other people feel they are stuck behind a screen rather than enjoying the variety of jobs in the pre-computer era.

LF IT is a labour-saving device, and like labour-saving devices in general, it has conspicuously failed to save labour. This is not to say we would be better off without it. There is a clear sense in which IT makes innumerable tasks quicker and easier, and thus expands the limits of what we are able to do. It saves labour in that sense. But under the present social conditions, at least, it does not save labour in the sense of allowing us to work less hard, or for less long – we just get certain things done faster (other things slower), and perform endless other tasks, many of them made necessary by the same technology which had sped up the more traditional ones. Of course technology changes the way we work, but it does not do so in a vacuum: how it changes the way we work depends on the kind of society we have.

JM Everybody is aware that the use of technology has changed the way we work. People feel the

constant urge to respond to the never-ending in-flow of messages, especially in work cultures that demand instant responses, and they stay connected day and night, every day, every night. There are probably two psychological benefits to this: being in the loop gives people the good feeling that they are needed and it also keeps people busy. But these benefits come with costs: being unable to get out of the loop, at least for some periods of time, deprives people from the opportunity to rest and recover. It also prevents people from reflecting about what they are busy with. Often, what keeps us busy is not what makes us effective, and so a key to success is the ability to step back and reconsider whether what we are doing is the right thing to do. Perhaps, as technology develops, solutions will be found not only to connect people ever more, but also to intelligently disconnect people if there is a need to help them work more effectively.

Is the merging of work and leisure healthy?

BB Factories made life simpler than the agricultural work that preceded the Industrial Revolution or today's post-manufacturing era – people could only do paid work in the geographical and temporal limits of the working day inside the factory gates. Now mobile devices 'allow' more of us to work anywhere and anytime. For some of us this is a great advantage, permitting a better accommodation between employment and other activities, such as childcare and leisure, while reducing the need to commute in rush-hours. Other people feel that it is increasingly hard to control their involvement in employment and they suffer from its spill-over into family and leisure time.

LF No. In a truly healthy society, we might not even mark much of a distinction between work and leisure, and so this question wouldn't arise. A sharp separation is not healthy, but nor is a 'merger' of a damaged version of 'work' (slog) and an equally damaged version of 'leisure' (consumption). To paraphrase a comment by the 1960s, psychiatrist RD Laing, there is no point trying to put a shattered Humpty-Dumpty back together. Answering e-mails in the pub does not make work any more leisure-like, and it certainly does nothing for the pub.

JM The merging of work and leisure can be healthy, especially in the era of the knowledge economy. People's best ideas for work-related issues often emerge during leisure activities, such as sport or simply relaxing in the sunshine. In addition, leisure time provides people the opportunity to think about their work, take stock of their current activities and then allocate their work time more effectively to high-priority tasks. The merging of work and leisure thus has benefits, but the problem is that too often there is no merging – instead work eats up all the leisure time. That then is problematic, because it robs people of the opportunity to have creative ideas, which is counterproductive in knowledge-driven jobs. One solution to this is to make work more leisurely. The company Sonova, a Swiss producer of hearing aids, deliberately builds into the work allocation system leisure periods that follow intense work periods. Microsoft's Bill Gates used to take 'think weeks' in his cottage twice a year, during which he evaluated ideas submitted by his employees. Getting away from the day-to-day business helped him recharge while getting one of the most important business tasks done. Today, dozens of Microsoft's big thinkers follow this pattern. These examples show that the merging has to go both ways to be healthy.

Some people have too much work; others have none. What's the solution?

BB When surveys ask people how much paid work they would ideally like to do (for a given hourly rate of pay), the unemployed and part-time employees say they would want more hours of employment, and full-timers say they want less; most people seem to converge on a four-day week as being optimal. There is no sign that 'market forces' will take us any nearer to this favoured solution. Competition in our careers for promotion and for material goods (e.g. houses) seems to create a very unhealthy inequality in the distribution of work. We need a combination of regulations and intelligent policies to nudge us to a less unequal distribution of work. But that's not easy – policy makers and researchers are going to have to be smart to help solve this problem.

LF Revolution. This is a word which means importantly different things to different people. But on any permissible understanding, it implies a fundamental change in the way we organise the economy and society – not just the adoption of various measures to mitigate the worst effects of the system we now have.

JM The distribution of work is – and always will be – an economic and societal challenge. As a management scholar, I can say that in organisations, when people work too much it is sometimes not the best solution simply to hire new people to distribute work more broadly. Often, too much work results from a lack of strategic focus – the 'multi-loading' I have described. People work day and night, because everything seems important to them and their managers give them a plethora of goals to meet. This diffusion in focus distracts – and sometime prevents – people from reaching the best outcome to the most important tasks. Therefore, the question for organisations is first why people do the work they do, and then how many people should do the work. The solution for people working too much is to stop doing what is not essential – but I have noticed that it is often very difficult for people to let go of tasks, in part because they feel bad about not finishing something they started, because the tasks are parts of cherished routines, or quite simply because the tasks are more easily and quickly accomplished than the more essential ones.

How might our ways of working change over the next 30 years – and will we be happier and healthier?

BB I think that there has been a slow, albeit erratic, improvement in the quality of employment over the past two generations, as the workforce has become better educated and more able to do more skilled work. Recent economic crises have halted that progress, and increased job insecurity is a problem for many. It's important that we consider the sustainability of jobs if we expect people to work longer and retire later. I'm optimistic that the quality of jobs can continue to improve if governments, employers and trade unions prioritise this over economic growth. We also need to pay attention to the impact of our working lives on the environment if we want a happy and healthy future.

LF Given the effect of our 'ways of working' on the planet – the devastating effects of man-made climate change which are already beginning to be felt – many people cannot expect to be alive in 30 years' time, let alone happier or healthier.

JM People have become healthier and, perhaps, happier over recent decades, so I hope this trend will continue. Whether it does, depends on us. There are big challenges that lie ahead. Meeting them together as a society rather than alone as individuals could provide a pleasant sense of collective progress for us all – but too often it seems as if only a few progress and others are left behind. If we found a way of working together more effectively and sustainably, and of distributing the outcomes of our work more fairly, I think we will get closer to the worthy goals of health and happiness.

6 September 2013

⇨ The above information is reprinted with kind permission from the University of Cambridge, Dr Brendan Burchell, Lorna Finlayson and Dr Jochen Menges. Please visit www.cam.ac.uk for further information.

© University of Cambridge 2013

Key facts

- The 1950s and 1960s saw a very low rate of unemployment (around three per cent on average) as a result of the 'postwar boom'. (page 1)

- In 1982 unemployment topped three million. (page 1)

- In May 2010, when the Coalition came to power unemployment was 2.5 million. (page 2)

- There were 147,000 redundancies in March to May 2012, down 27,000 on the previous quarter but up 4,000 on the year. (page 3)

- 20.3 million families in Britain receive some kind of benefit. This is equal to 64% of all families. (page 6)

- Around 58,000 households will have their benefits reduced in 2014–15. (page 7)

- Out of 2.8 million workless households of working age, 2.5 million will see their entitlements reduced by an average of about £215 a year in 2015–16. (page 7)

- Since 2008, 878,000 new employment and support allowance claims have been closed before the claimant was able to be assessed and 729,000 have been found 'fit to work' by tests. (page 8)

- The world's richest 85 people, who could all fit on a double decker bus, own as much as the world's poorest 3.5 billion. (page 12)

- In Greece, over 80 per cent of all housework is done by women and for those women working 30 hours or more per week, more than three-quarters of them still have responsibility for household chores. (page 15)

- By 2020, a third of the UK's workforce will be over 50. (page 16)

- Nearly 1.5 million young people are currently not in education, employment or training. This equates to over one in five of all young people. (page 19)

- 5.6 million young people are unemployed across Europe. (page 21)

- Major new research with over 18,000 final year university students from the 'Class of 2013' confirms that finalists who had completed an internship or other vacation work with employers during their studies were three times more likely to receive a definite job offer before leaving university, compared with undergraduates who'd done no work experience at all. (page 24)

- 26% of final-year students hope to go on to postgraduate study. (page 24)

- 70% of students began researching their career options before the beginning of their final year at university. (page 24)

- Just 56% of employers report they are likely to recruit young people within the next 12 months. In all, 58% of private sector employers say they are likely to recruit young people over the next year. (page 26)

- Nearly two-thirds of employers think they can help young people by providing career insights in the classroom through school visits and talks to schoolchildren. (page 27)

- Two in ten workers perceive older workers to have more accidents at work than other workers. (page 31)

- Unacceptable behaviours such as bullying or harassment are perceived as a common cause of work-related stress by six in ten workers (59%). (page 31)

- 74% of British workers feel burned out in the current job. (page 32)

- 40% of British workers plan to change jobs in the next 12 months. (page 32)

- Around three in ten (28%) think that older workers aged 60+ are less productive at work than other workers. (page 32)

- Four in ten (42%) think that older workers tend to suffer more from work-related stress than other workers. (page 32)

Apprenticeship

A scheme where firms take on workers for an initial training period. They can then go on to become full-time employees once they have developed the necessary skills. Apprentices learn and gain qualifications on the job and receive a weekly wage.

Equality Bill

The Equality Bill is expected to come into force from autumn 2010 (subject to successfully passing through Parliament). The Bill sets out groundbreaking new laws which will help narrow the gap between rich and poor; require business to report on gender pay; outlaw age discrimination; and will significantly strengthen Britain's anti-discrimination legislation.

Flexible working

Any working pattern which allows an individual to vary the time or place in which work is done. Flexible working schemes include part-time work, flexitime and job sharing.

Labour market

The market in which workers compete for jobs and employers compete for workers.

Maternity leave

Female employees have the statutory right to a minimum amount of time off during and following a pregnancy. Statutory maternity leave is currently 52 weeks. It is made up of 'Ordinary Maternity Leave' of 26 weeks and 'Additional Maternity Leave' of 26 weeks.

Minimum wage

The National Minimum Wage (NMW) is a minimum amount per hour that most workers in the UK are legally entitled to be paid. The level of NMW you are entitled to depends on your age.

NEET

Young people not in employment, education or training.

Pension

A regular payment made to people who have retired from work. State pension is paid by the government to those who have qualifying years from their National Insurance (NI) contributions record. The age when you may be able to claim state pension is currently 65 for men and 60 for women. You can also set up a personal pension, which are available from banks, building societies and life insurance companies who will invest your savings on your behalf. Company pensions are set up by employers to provide pensions for their employees upon retirement.

Recession

A period during which economic activity has slowed, causing a reduction in Gross Domestic Product (GDP), employment, household incomes and business profits. If GDP shows a reduction over at least six months, a country is then said to be in recession.

Retirement

Stopping work. People who retire once they have reached State Pension age can claim their pension, which provides a regular income for the rest of their life.

Work-life balance

Having a measure of control over when, where and how you work, in order to enjoy an optimal quality of life. In a 2008 survey of Oxbridge graduates, a majority in every sector said they would prioritise work-life balance when thinking about their career.

Vocational

A qualification which is relevant to a particular career and can be expected to provide a route into that career. Examples are qualifications in accountancy or journalism. This differs from an academic qualification, which focuses on a particular academic subject.

Assignments

Brainstorming

⇨ With a partner, discuss what you know about unemployment in the UK. Draw a mind-map of all the things you think about in connection with the issue of unemployment.

⇨ In small groups, think about the different types of career paths people might follow after they leave school. List as many careers as you can think of, and include a note that explains whether each job requires a degree, A-levels, GCSEs, work experience, an apprenticeship, a college course, etc.

Research

⇨ In pairs, create a five-minute PowerPoint presentation that explores how unemployment in the UK has changed since the 1950s. You might like to talk to your parents or grandparents and ask about their experiences.

⇨ Research they way in which attitudes to women in the workplace have changed since the 1950s. Write some notes on your findings and feedback to the rest of the class.

⇨ Choose a country outside of the EU and research their attitude to work and employment. Write some notes on your findings and feedback to your class.

Design

⇨ Using the article on page four, *Rights at work*, create a booklet that explains a worker's statutory rights at work.

⇨ Design a poster that will encourage people who are unemployed and not currently seeking work, to look for employment.

⇨ In small groups, imagine that you work for a company that runs team-building activities for large companies. In your group, plan a day that will encourage employees to deal with work-place stress. Create a leaflet that describes your stress-busting activity day and detail what is involved. You might like to think of a name and a logo to accompany your idea.

⇨ Design an app that would help people who are out of work find voluntary or paid placements relevant to their desired field of employment.

Oral

⇨ In small groups, research the current welfare system in the UK. Now, imagine that you are setting up your own political party. Decide what you would change, and what you would keep the same, about the welfare system and deliver a speech detailing your policies. Try to make your speech persuasive – remember you are trying to convince people that your policies are better than anyone else's.

⇨ The article on page 16 says that 'people with disabilities or long-term illnesses… are more likely to fall into unemployment'. With a partner, discuss why you think this is, and what could be done to help these people find work.

⇨ Think about a job you would like to do in the future and create a five minute presentation that explores the qualifications and experience you might need in order to enter that profession.

Reading/writing

⇨ Read the article *The National Minimum Wage* on page five. Calculate how much money a 24-year-old would make, per week, if they worked 35 hours and were paid the National Minimum Wage. Create a budget detailing what you would spend on rent, food, bills and leisure expenses.

⇨ Read the article *Benefits in Britain: separating the facts from the fiction* on page six. Create a bullet point list which summarises the article's key points.

⇨ Imagine that you are a young person who has decided to start their own business after struggling to find work. Write an outline for a business plan which details your business idea, your start-up costs and why you think it will be successful.

⇨ Imagine that you are a single parent with two children who currently works 9am–5pm in an office environment. You are finding it increasingly difficult to manage taking your children to and from school with your current working pattern. Write a letter to your employer, requesting flexible working conditions. See the article on page 33 for guidance.

⇨ Read the article on page 30 *Sherlock Holmes museum curator scorns 'lazy' job applicant for vacancy enquiry*. Think about what the museum curator should have said in her letter, and write your own version that is more helpful and polite.

⇨ Watch the 2006 film, starring Will Smith, *The Pursuit of Happyness* and write a report exploring the theme of employment in the film.

Acknowledgements

The publisher is grateful for permission to reproduce the material in this book. While every care has been taken to trace and acknowledge copyright, the publisher tenders its apology for any accidental infringement or where copyright has proved untraceable. The publisher would be pleased to come to a suitable arrangement in any such case with the rightful owner.

Images

Cover, page iii and page 37: iStock, page 2 © Elisabetta Focco, page 7: iStock, page 10: MorgueFile, page 14: iStock, page 16: iStock, page 17: iStock, page 20 © Jackie Staines, pages 24 and 25 © iStock.

Illustrations

Don Hatcher: pages 1 & 36. Simon Kneebone: pages 8 & 26. Angelo Madrid: pages 4 & 33.

Additional acknowledgements

Editorial on behalf of Independence Educational Publishers by Cara Acred.

With thanks to the Independence team: Mary Chapman, Sandra Dennis, Christina Hughes, Jackie Staines and Jan Sunderland.

Cara Acred

Cambridge, May 2014